Anger Management:

13 Powerful Steps to Take Complete Control of Your Emotions, For Men and Women, Self-Help Guide for Self Control, Psychology Behind Anger

Table of Contents

Introduction......8

Chapter 1: Anger......10

Negative Thought Patterns
Expression of Anger
Other Anger Expression Methods
Understanding Anger
Physiology of Anger
Smart Anger

Chapter 2: Causes of Anger......24

Anger at a Young Age
Anger Through Generations
Acquisition of Anger Styles
Anger and Gender
Anger and Culture
Populations Affected by Anger

- Adults
- Children and Adolescents
- Individuals with Intellectual Disabilities
- Violent Criminals
- Substance Abusers
- Post-Traumatic Stress Disorder

Chapter 3: Signs and Symptoms of Anger-Related Issues......36

Chronic Anger
Emotional Symptoms of Problems Related to Anger
Physical Symptoms of Problems Related to Anger

Chapter 4: The Costs of Anger......45

Health Costs

- Blood Pressure and Heart Disease
- Personality Types and Anger

Social Costs
Motivational Costs and Effects of Anger

Chapter 5: Anger and Mental Health......51

The Connection Between Anger and Stress
Quick Tips for Managing Stress and Anger
The Impact of Anger and Stress
Anger and Your Beliefs
The Iceberg
Anger, Alcohol, and Drug Abuse

Chapter 6: The Choice to Manage Anger......63

The Stages of Change
Mandatory Anger Management Treatment
Why You Have to Stay Cool
The Major Challenges Hindering the Cultivation of Healthy Anger

1. The underestimation of the work that it will take to change
2. Anger towards the amount of effort needed for change
3. Anger normally works in the short-term.
4. Discomfort in reflection
5. Thinking and feeling that one needs to change habits are two different things.
6. Familiarity
7. The tension that accompanies applying new skills
8. The rewarding feeling that accompanies anger
9. Using anger to avoid responsibility
10. Concentrating on the activities that are rewarding in the short term
11. Mental disorders

Chapter 7: Steps to Managing Anger Effectively......76

Using an Anger Diary
Anger Management Relaxation Techniques

Controlled deep breathing
Practicing slow breathing
Progressive muscle relaxation

Reality Testing as an Anger Management Tool

Reality Testing
Black-and-white thinking
Talking it out helps
Count to ten

Chapter 8: Anger Management and Communication......90

Anger Management and Request Making

Chapter 9: Selecting an Anger Management Program......96

Individual and Group Therapy
Anger Management Classes
Self-Study
Following Through the Anger Management Program
Cognitive Behavioral Therapy for Anger Management

Cognitive Behavioral Therapy – Goal-Oriented
Cognitive Behavioral Therapy – Focused on the Present
Cognitive Behavioral Therapy – Active
Cognitive Behavioral Therapy – Brief
Cognitive Behavioral Therapy – Well-Researched

Other Treatment Program Options
Residential / Inpatient Anger Management Treatment Programs

Benefits of In-House Anger Management Treatments

Executive Anger Management Program
Outpatient Anger Treatment Programs
Finding the Best Anger Management Treatment Facility
The Contractual Commitment

Take some time out

Examining thought
Assertive communication
Contract duration
Let people help you
Reward yourself

Chapter 10: The Use of Anger Management Techniques: Putting Them Together......116

Practice Makes It Perfect
Anger and Advocacy

Chapter 11: Relapses and Anger Treatment.....122

Mentality About Relapses

Stick to your plan.
Seek feedback.
Incentivize yourself.
Warning Signs of a Relapse

Chapter 12: Anger Medication and Side Effects......129

Common Medications

Anti-Depressants
Mood Stabilizers
Antipsychotic Drugs

The Safety of Medication Treatment

Chapter 13: Summary of Anger Management Techniques......132

Feeling Angry
What to Do
Immediate Strategies
Short-Term Strategies
Longer-Term Strategies

Conclusion......139

© Copyright 2019 by Tony Bennis - All rights reserved.

This Book is provided with the sole purpose of providing relevant information on a specific topic for which every reasonable effort has been made to ensure that it is both accurate and reasonable. Nevertheless, by purchasing this Book you consent to the fact that the author, as well as the publisher, are in no way experts on the topics contained herein, regardless of any claims as such that may be made within. As such, any suggestions or recommendations that are made within are done so purely for entertainment value. It is recommended that you always consult a professional prior to undertaking any of the advice or techniques discussed within.

This is a legally binding declaration that is considered both valid and fair by both the Committee of Publishers Association and the American Bar Association and should be considered as legally binding within the United States.

The reproduction, transmission, and duplication of any of the content found herein, including any specific or extended information will be done as an illegal act regardless of the end form the information ultimately takes. This includes copied versions of the work both physical, digital and audio unless express consent of the Publisher is provided beforehand. Any additional rights reserved.

Furthermore, the information that can be found within the pages described forthwith shall be considered both accurate and truthful when it comes to the recounting of facts. As such, any use, correct or incorrect, of the provided information will render the Publisher free of responsibility as to the actions taken outside of their direct purview.

Regardless, there are zero scenarios where the original author or the Publisher can be deemed liable in any fashion for any damages or hardships that may result from any of the information discussed herein.

Additionally, the information in the following pages is intended only for informational purposes and should thus be thought of as universal. As befitting its nature, it is presented without assurance regarding its prolonged validity or interim quality. Trademarks that are mentioned are done without written consent and can in no way be considered an endorsement from the trademark holder.

Introduction

Congratulations on downloading *Anger Management*, and thank you for doing so! Anger is part of human emotions designed to warn us of certain situations. This emotion can result from frustration, stress, loss, disrespect, poor relations, poverty, etc. Anger can scare anyone, especially if it becomes overwhelming and unmanaged, as it can make a person act irrationally. In most cases, we have been taught that anger is a dangerous emotion and should be avoided. However, it is very challenging to avoid anger in this life because we have experienced certain things that make us offensive or defensive and alert.

Anger is a natural occurrence, but how we react to it is a choice. Our reactions are either voluntary or involuntary. Uncontrolled anger can be dangerous—it impedes the decision-making ability of an individual, damages relations, destroys careers, and other adverse consequences. As such, it is essential for one to understand the anger and the ways that he or she can manage it. Anger management is the ability to prevent or control anger successfully so that it does not lead to problems.

To that end, this book will discuss anger, its effects, and practices that a person may apply to manage anger. The information you find in this book can be practiced as soon as a person desires. The first chapter will cover the introduction to anger, expression of anger, understanding anger, and smart anger, among others. Chapter 2 and 3 will cover the causes, signs, and symptoms of anger and unmanaged anger. Chapters 4, 5, and 6 will cover the cost of anger, anger and mental health, and the choice to manage anger. Chapter 7, 8, and 9 will talk about steps to managing anger effectively, anger management and communication, and ways to select a good anger management program. Chapter 10, 11, and, 12 will cover the use of anger management techniques, relapses, and medication. Finally, Chapter 13 will summarize the anger management techniques.

Chapter 1: Anger

At one point or the other, everybody feels angry. In some occasions, people perceive it as a temporary annoyance— while other times, they experience it as a fully-fledged rage. Anger is a normal part of human life, and it *is* healthy. The emotion helps us discern moments when we are offended when things are not working as we planned or hoped. It gives us a way to express negative feelings, and it motivates us to find solutions for challenges.

Although anger is good and healthy, it can be destructive when it gets out of control. Problems may arise at work, in relationships, and the wholesome quality of life. Uncontrolled anger can make one feel like he/she is at the mercy of a powerful and unpredictable emotion. Consequently, many people look for ways to control anger. The intensity of the emotional state of anger varies from mild to complete rage and fury. Physical and psychological changes accompany it. For instance, when one is angry, the heartbeat rate changes; blood pressure goes up; the levels of energies change, depending on the situation; and hormones, adrenaline, and noradrenaline are altered.

Anger may arise from either internal or external events. For instance, one may be angry because of a traffic jam, failure to do a particular thing, cancellation of a flight, bullying, loss, humiliation, etc. Internally, anger may arise because one feels that he/she is worrying or brooding too much about personal problems, is frustrated because of failure, etc. Feelings of anger also arise because of things that occurred to a person in the past—for instance, traumatic events during childhood years. Anger is usually characterized by conflict towards a person or a thing because of a particular wrongful thing done towards the person.

Negative Thought Patterns

Typically, anger has less to do with the immediate event and more to do with our reaction towards the event. Specific negative thought patterns often precede an outburst of rage. These patterns include:

Overgeneralizing - This pattern occurs when one is stuck in black and white thinking. He/she thinks of only what is visible immediately. People caught up in this pattern tend to use words like 'never' and 'always.' Overgeneralizing makes a situation appear to be worse than it is.

Blaming - Blaming involves a person claiming that negative emotions or events are the faults of someone else. In most cases, a person accuses the other when trying to avoid shame or responsibility.

Mind reading - This involves a person getting convinced that the other is hurting them intentionally. The person may imagine hostility when there is none. Angry people will see danger where they would not imagine under normal circumstances.

Rigidity - This occurs when one is not able to reconcile the happening events with what they imagined. For instance, one may have assumed that he/she will get to the office by 8 am, but a traffic jam hinders them. Instead if accepting that they are late, an angry person will get angered and probably stay in an awful mood for an extended period.

Collecting straws - This involves a scenario where an angry person mentally counts things in an attempt to justify anger. Consequently, the person will allow a series of small incidents to build up in their head until the last straw is broken.
Challenging these thoughts can help a person to reduce anger.

Expression of Anger

People use different ways to express anger. The most intuitive and natural way of expressing anger is aggression. Majority of people react aggressively to people or things that anger them. This is because; anger is designed to help human beings respond to threats and certain unwanted situations. As such, the emotion inspires power/strength which generally comes off as aggression more so if the individual lacks knowledge of how to control it. These feelings and behaviors allow us to defend ourselves, fight, and find solutions for our challenges. We can, therefore, say that a certain level of anger is necessary for human survival.

However, we cannot respond to every other person and thing aggressively or physically just because we are angry. There are societal norms, laws, and logic that limit the way we behave under certain circumstances. The situation and circumstances (people involved, time, place, reason etc.) determine the way we react. For example, in an office setting, it would be hard for one to go off on the boss even if he/she is stepping on the toes of every other person. It would also be hard to talk to grandparents however we like just because we are angry.

People use both unconscious and conscious processes to deal with their anger. There are three main approaches referred to as suppressing, expressing and calming. Researches show that the best (healthiest) way for one to deal with anger is to show the emotion assertively and not aggressively. To adequately express anger assertively, one needs to learn what their needs are and state it clearly without hurting others. Assertiveness does not mean pushy or too much demand; preferably, it means doing things in a way that is respectful to others.

One can also suppress anger, then convert or redirect it to something positive. Anger suppression occurs when one holds in the anger, avoids thinking about it, and focuses on something nice. The bottom line of suppression is to inhibit anger and convert it into constructive things. However, there is a challenge that occurs with anger suppression if not managed well. If there lacks an outward expression, one might turn the anger inwards and blame self. Suppressed anger has been identified as an underlying cause of depression and anxiety. Unexpressed anger can disrupt relationships, affect behavior patterns and thinking, and also create an array of physical problems. Anger that is turned inwards can lead to high blood pressure, hypertension, and depression.

Unexpressed anger also leads to other problems. One possible consequence of rage is the pathological expression of the emotion, for instance through passive-aggressive behavior or a personality that is ordinarily hostile or cynical. Passive-aggressive behavior refers to the patterns of continually getting back at people indirectly without telling them the reason. People with passive-aggressive behavior will avoid confrontation. People who like criticizing everything, putting others down, or making cynical comments now and then have not learned ways to deal with anger constructively. As such, these people are less likely to have successful relationships.

Calming down is the most successful way of dealing with anger. Calming down the insides means that one does not control just the outward behavior but also the internal responses. Calming down techniques allow one to lower the heartbeat rate and other physical changes and let the feelings subside. When one is unable to use any of the three techniques (expressing, suppressing, or calming) constructively, then anger becomes harmful.

Other Anger Expression Methods

How we express anger determines our health and the wellness of other people around us. It is therefore vital to understand the different ways through which anger is shown and how we can choose better expression skills. Apart from the main expression, suppression and calming down methods, there are other ways that people use to show their displeasure. They include:

Open aggression - Open aggression involves a situation where one expresses anger through actions and words more so through blame, intimidation, explosiveness, and rage. The challenge with these techniques is that there are high chances of causing damage to the other person. In fact, the main aim of the people that use this option is to cause harm to the other person (intimidating others). In the end, everyone in the picture gets to experience recurring power struggles.

Passive aggression - In this option, the person does not rely on open hostility; instead, he/she prefers to use subtle sabotage to frustrate others or get revenge. It usually involves failing to do someone a favor because of the will to irritate him/her. The similarity between the open aggressor and passive aggressor is that the two persons compete for superiority. Both situations perpetuate unwanted tension and usually generate unhealthy relationships. As such, the passive aggression choice will result in another undesirable conflict.

Assertive anger - The expression of anger typically involves words and actions that show respect and dignity for everyone in the situation. The people who use this style understand that the tone of voice used in any situation will either create a positive or a negative atmosphere. Essentially, it is not always easy for one to express anger in assertively, but with self-discipline and a lot of respect, it is manageable. Remember that assertive anger is not abrasive pushy; instead, it is strong and respectful. Confidently expressing anger is an option that is very constructive and reduces tension in every relationship.

Dropping anger - This option is almost similar to calming down style. The angry person accepts that the other methods of expressing anger will not work therefore chooses to let the matter go. Normally, the persons opting for assertive anger are the ones who decide to drop it. The aggressive people want to pick the fight to the end, but assertive people look for ways to resolve conflicts with least altercations. Dropping anger is not easy, and it includes accommodating the differences and choosing to forgive even without receiving an apology.

Conclusively, many occasions in life lead to anger every day. As such, it is difficult to manage anger using only one option. However, with practice, we can choose and stick to an anger expression option that improves the wellness of everyone around us.

Understanding Anger

Anger is also referred to as fury, wrath or rage. It is an emotion that should not be underestimated. It frequently occurs for some people and rarely for others, but in most cases, its consequences are very unhelpful. Anger is a natural experience for many people, and sometimes, everyone has valid reasons to get furious or mad. If someone says something that feels unfair to the other, then there might be a compelling reason to get mad.

The major cause of anger is the environment that one is spending time. Financial issues, stress, poor social and family situation, abuse, and other overwhelming requirements on time and energy may contribute to the occurrence of anger.

Anger disorders might be prevalent in people coming from families with the same challenges similar to the way people are more prone to alcoholism if they grew in families with the disorder. The ability of the body to deal with certain hormones and chemicals and genetics also play a role in the way one deals with anger. If the brain of an individual does not react in a healthy way to serotonin, he/she might find it harder to manage the emotions.

Anger takes different forms in different people, for instance, some will stay mad for an extended period because of an event that took place a long time ago, but they will do nothing serious out of the emotion. Others will stay for a very long period without getting angry but once they do, it outs as explosive bouts of rage.

Regardless of the shape taken by the anger, any uncontrolled emotion will affect the emotional wellbeing and physical health of the individual. According to researches, unchecked anger and hostility increase the chances of one developing coronary heart diseases and makes the situations worse for the people suffering from heart diseases. Anger also results in problems that are stress related such as insomnia, headaches, and digestive issues. Anger may also result in risky and violent behavior including fights, and drug and substance abuse. Additionally, anger can cause significant damage to relationships in families, among friends and with colleagues.

Physiology of Anger

Like any other emotion, anger has effects on our minds and bodies. Scientists have found a series of biological events that take place as we become angry. According to researches, emotions tend to begin inside our brains in two almond-shaped structures called the Amygdala. The amygdala is responsible for spotting the things and situations that threaten out wellbeing, therefore, setting off an alarm for us to defend ourselves. Once the warning is off, we take the necessary steps to protect our interests. This section of the brain is so useful that it gets us to act before we can think clearly.

The cortex part of the brain is responsible for judgment and thought therefore in charge of checking the reasonableness of a reaction before it is taken. When angry, the cortex does not act fast enough. In simple terms, the brain is wired to influence our acts before we can even consider the consequence of our deeds. However, this should not be a reason for us to behave in the wrong way – we can learn to control aggressive impulses with time and patience. Proper management of anger is a skill that one must choose to learn; it is not something that people are born with instinctually.

As you become angry, the muscles in your body tense up. In the brain, a neurotransmitter chemical referred to as catecholamine is released resulting in an experience of energy burst lasting up to several minutes. That energy burst is the main reason why anger is accompanied by an immediate desire to take protective action. Simultaneously, the heartbeat rate accelerates, the blood pressure rises, and the breathing rate increases. Some people experience flushes in the face as the increased blood flow accesses the extremities and limbs as the body prepares for physical action.

In the moment of anger, the attention of a person becomes narrow and locked on the target. Soon, one is unable to pay attention to any other thing. Quickly, additional hormones more so the adrenal and noradrenaline, and brain neurotransmitters are released thus triggering a full state of arousal. At that point, one is ready to fight.

Since the body has a preparation process when one is angry, it also has a calming down process. Once the source of our threat is no longer accessible, or the immediate threat is gone, we start to relax and get back to our normal resting state. It is hard to relax when you already are in an angry state. The arousal that results from adrenaline rush lasts for a long time. For some people, the arousal may last for a few hours while some experience it for a day or more. That extended state of arousal makes it easy for one to get angry quickly again even after the initial situation is gone. It takes a long time for one to return to a completely normal resting state. During the slow process of cooling down, one is more likely to lose temper in response to a small irritation that would not bother us.

This lingering arousal also interferes with our memory, and that is why we forget the events that took place during the outburst. The linger keeps us ready for more anger. We cannot defy the arousal because it is essential for the functionality of the brain. Without the arousal, we would most probably be forever sleepy. Any student knows that it is almost impossible for one to grasp new matter when sleepy. Moderate arousal enhances memory and helps the brain to learn, perform, and concentrate. The form of arousal occurring during anger moments is too much and thus makes it hard to develop new memories. Loss of memory is one of the disadvantages of uncontrolled anger.

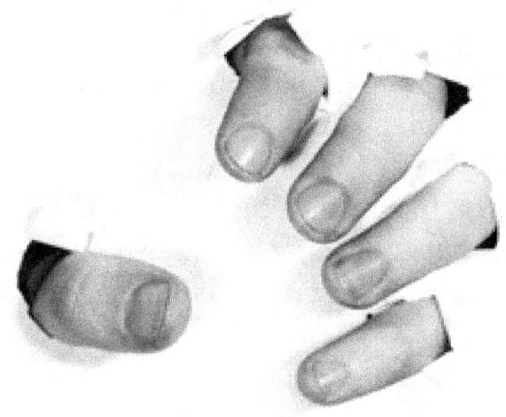

Smart Anger

Many people seek for ways to deal with anger because they find it unpleasant and in most cases, it results in negative implications. What we do when angry determines a lot of things in the future. Because most anger ends up with negative consequences, we tend to assume that anger is bad. Many people have been taught that anger is a dangerous emotion which should be ignored or suppressed by all means. In most cases, the female gender is discouraged from showing anger because it is defined as unladylike. Cultures have taught us that anger is a display of arrogance. We have also observed people getting angry and seen what they ended up doing.

Because anger involves pain and confusion, it can lead to actions that cause problems. As such, we choose to focus on ways of suppressing, avoiding, or minimizing anger. It is rare to find someone who views anger as an enjoyable and fulfilling emotion. Majority of us see it as a problem, a thing we should get rid of. However, anger has a purpose in our lives, and it is useful. Emotional pain might seem unnecessary in our lives, but like physical pain, it serves a vital role in our lives. If you burn your finger, you will withdraw from the thing that is burning it and give it time to heal. Similarly, emotions such as anger send us a message.

In particular, anger warns us that something is wrong and we should stand, find solutions, and overcome the obstacles. True, our actions when we are angry can result in regrets. Acting in an aggressive manner is not a smart thing to do whether we are justified to be angry or not. We feel bad after an outburst. Typically, when in danger, our bodies are designed to act before thinking critically; therefore, we can be quite irrational when in danger. However, we do not have to be out of control when angry. It is possible for one to think clearly, analyze, and understand the provocative situation. Then, he/she will be able to use emotion as motivation to initiate positive change.

There are two mistakes that people make when it comes to anger. They either try to be happy in the hurtful situation or try to ignore the feeling entirely. However, accepting and embracing the usefulness of anger improves the ability to think and act while emotional. Although it may seem contradictory, the desire to feel angry when facing a conflict will help you to understand and manage your emotions and situations.

Normally, we all want to feel good and avoid any bad feelings, but in some cases, unpleasant feelings are very beneficial. It is important to experience emotions that are congruent with our circumstances even though they are not pleasant. Of more value is the ability to understand and manage the emotions. Good ability to manage emotions is linked to better physical and emotional well-being.

The problem with anger is distinguishing the useful form from the unhelpful one. Hanging on to resentment long after the angering situation is gone leads to bad anger. Such anger will only make us vulnerable to more anger.

How then do we identify and apply useful anger in a smart way? First, assume that you are wrong about the situation; your reason for being angry is not valid. Breath, count, and breath until you feel rational. Controlling anger does not mean that you suppress it. Also, do not take actions that could amplify your anger. For instance, do not over-focus on the person or thing angering you. Look for a diversion. Then, analyze the events. Is the anger doing you any good? What message is it trying to pass to you? Are you being warned about injustice, disrespect, or loss? Is it motivating you to find a solution to a situation at work? Look at your past? Help the people around you or a particularly disadvantaged group? When you stop pushing away good anger, you will be able to make choices about your responses to life.

Chapter 2: Causes of Anger

Anger at a Young Age

From a very tender age, people experience this fundamental emotion called anger and learn to express it depending on the people they see around them. Young children will express anger depending on what they copy from the adults and the reward they get for it. Generally, the world has an uneasy relationship with the expression of anger—therefore, we grow up thinking that it is wrong to express anger directly. We are taught that anger is a dangerous emotion at all times and that it should not be tolerated. Consequently, most of us learn how to ignore/suppress anger, distrust the feeling, bottle everything up, and only use it in very indirect ways. The danger with ignoring anger is that it only wells up inside of us and blows up at one point or the other.

It is true to say that anger can be very destructive when mismanaged, but it has a list of advantages. When used well, anger becomes more than just a destructive force.
Anger is a very important part of self-defense and self-preservation instincts. If we were entirely unable to get angry, then it would be hard to stand for ourselves. People would offend us over and over again yet we would do nothing about it. It is therefore very important that we learn the ways through which we can express anger effectively. There are healthy and socially respectful strategies that one can use to express the feelings of anger. It is important to express these feelings in a controlled way in order to preserve our relationships, health, and employability.

Anger Through Generations

Anger can be passed down from one person to the other in a family. However, there lacks substantial evidence showing that anger can be passed through genes. It is only learned or acquired. People think that anger is genetic because they can remember someone in the family line that was pretty angry and irritable—maybe a parent, grandparent, or another relative. Anger is an acquired behavior that sticks with practice. The only exception is the anger occurring due to other mental disorders and illnesses.

Family determines how one expresses emotions such as happiness, sadness, fear, anger etc. If anger was not handled properly by the grandparents, chances are, the parents will be angry and so will the children. Please note, there is no deal parent. Every person is flawed, and so are parents. There are flaws inherited by your parents from their parents, and you will probably gather some from them, involuntarily. Anger is to some extent passed on from generation to the next. It is up to you to recognize the behaviors you would rather not pass to your children. Drop the unhelpful and hurtful habits.

How can you protect your children from inheriting anger management issues and other wrong habits? First, keep in mind the fact that you are a role model. You are probably the first and main example your children will learn anything from, therefore, be alert. If you can learn how to break bad anger management habits, then you can break the chain. The bottom line is to cut off the wrong chains. Just think how beautiful it would be if your family could lead a better life; full of success and calmness.

When family members become angry, take time to talk to, and with them about their feelings. Keep in mind that anger is hardly the primary feeling. Look for signs of depression, fear, anxiety, sadness or other root emotions. When the children positively handle their anger, reward them. If they don't, talk to them and if the problem continues, seek professional help. To help your family:

- Look for appropriate ways to communicate with your partner, children, and other relatives; assertive communication can help.
- Always manage your anger regardless of the circumstance.
- Educate your children about anger.
- Discuss the best methods of coping with anger in the family.
- Participate in family therapy and formulate an anger management plan with the members.
- For the family members who still have challenges, recommend individual anger therapy.

Acquisition of Anger Styles

Everybody is born with the emotion of anger, but no one is born with aggressive and chronic anger. Generally, everyone will respond to an abusive or frustrating situation in the way they see most viable, but it is based on the habits they learned. For instance, people who grew up in violent homes are more likely to have some inappropriate ways of handling frustrating situations. People who grew in homes where anger was handled properly will have an easier time dealing with others.

Aggressive response styles and chronic anger are normally learned. There are a variety of ways through which one can learn aggressive anger expression styles. Some people will pick the habits up from childhood by watching the behavior of older people around them. If the parents and people influencing them are angry, hostile, and constantly make threats, then the children will pick up on those habits. Even if the children do not show these habits at a young age, chances are, they will apply them at a later age, once they are around people they can intimidate. You will notice that these children have a hard time keeping friends and relationships because they intimidate and belittle others. One of the main challenges facing the people who picked anger from a tender age is that they might not realize their anger problem. For them, anger is just a normal thing they saw while growing up.

Anger victims have a desire for revenge and mastery; therefore, will doubtlessly develop anger problems. If a child spent a lot of time in an abusive situation, he/she might swear never to be vulnerable again and will do anything to deal with people who pose a threat. These children will start becoming hostile towards others building on the theory that 'a good offense is the best defense. This explains part of the bullying in schools. Alternatively, wounded or abused people may overgeneralize and look to revenge against an entire group of people while it is only a section of them who hurt them. An example of such anger is how some people hold prejudice against all immigrants from some countries that were enemies with their country.

Another way that angry people learn to be aggressive and hostile is through getting an award for being a bully. If one gets respect or seems to instill fear in other people because of their aggressive actions, then he/she gets motivated to continue with their anger display. Aggressive behavior will still go on if the person gets a raise in position and social status.

Anger and Gender

For a long time, people have assumed that men are angrier than women. It is thought that anger is a masculine emotion and Mars is full of short-tempered and angry men. Women are assumed to be calmer and graceful; Venus is full of love. Consequently, the world has accepted anger in men more than in women. Anger is unladylike, but for men, it represents power and dominance. Some phrases that support masculine anger include 'Men don't cry,' 'don't be like a girl' etc. As a result, men learn how to suppress their emotions.

Researches have revealed that men and women feel angry and there is no gender differentiation when it comes to that. Women get angry as intensely and as frequently as men. They even seek anger management help as many times or even more than men. The researchers that found differences in anger levels also state that women are angrier than men to a certain extent. However, these researches are not qualified. Majority of women have reported that they get angry, yell, feel annoyed, and lose their temper. Men, on the other hand, stated that they prefer to keep their emotions. They are forced to suppress them and will only act out when pushed to the farthest edge.

Other researches have revealed that although there is no difference in the frequency of anger based on gender, women tend to dwell on the issue that angered them for longer, report more intense anger episodes, and discuss their anger more openly. The reason for dwelling on the anger for longer is the intensity. Women tend to feel things more deeply than men, thus will broad on a subject matter more. Again, women are more open therefore will openly discuss the things irritating them.

The differences between men and women cannot be seen in the term anger but are very evident in aggression. The feeling is almost similar, but the behavior differs. Men are more likely to involve physical action when angry than men. This remains almost consistent in time and culture because men are taught to be tough. On the other hand, women tend to employ effective and indirect modes of anger expression such as recruiting allies, gossiping, withdrawing affection, and crying. Often we interpret the reactions of women as being reasonable, but actually, it is because they are outsized by men; therefore, will play the hand they are dealt with. Women are more likely to express anger towards fellow women than men.

Gender may also influence the anger type that one typically possesses. Women will have the form of anger that shows resentment while men will have the type of anger that is revengeful. Women are also more likely to express anger towards themselves than to other people.

Anger and Culture

As mentioned earlier, we cannot always express anger as we want. The circumstance and people involved determine the ways through which we will sort our issues. The societal norms determine how we respond to the people we are angry at regardless of the emotion. Cultures have different rules about the expression of anger. There are display rules in every community that determines the ways that one can express anger appropriately. Researches have revealed patterns in display rules among individualist and collectivist cultures.

Individualist cultures stand for self-expression and independence. Their anger-display rules state that it is more appropriate to:

1. Minimize the expression of anger instead of elimination it all together.
2. Show your anger to friends and family rather than to strangers. People in individualist cultures tend to shift between groups; therefore, find it more important to maintain relations with people they do not know that family and friends. These people also rely less on a single group of social interactions.

Collectivist cultures prioritize group cohesion and cooperation. Their anger-display rules state that it is more appropriate to:

1. Stay in harmony. Harmony is important; therefore, you have to conceal anger too maintain it. People may show no emotion at all or mask their anger with other things.
2. Express your anger to strangers instead of family or friends. Some coping mechanisms of anger may be supported by one community and discouraged by another, and as such, one should consider their culture as they seek anger management help.

Populations Affected by Anger

Anger can affect anyone regardless of age gender or ethnicity. Anger is in most cases fueled by our beliefs, and exposure. If we are exposed to anger at a tender age, or the beliefs instilled in us are not rational, then we are more likely to be affected by the emotion.

Adults

Anger in adults normally affects the career and family life. One challenge that is extensively motivating adults to seek anger management help is career life. There are anger preventive and corrective tools available for individuals to cope with stress and anger stemming from job-related issues. For instance, people working with mentally challenged individuals are likely to experience stress when they have patients who are not improving. Consequently, they will have anger issues. Anger management skills have been developed to help such caretakers (for instance those working with people with dementia) cope with the feelings of frustration that might lead to anger. Other anger management programs are designed to help couples who have anger management challenges.

Children and Adolescents

The ability of a child to understand his/her emotions and how to react in particular situations can greatly determine the way he/she expresses anger. Sharing with young children the appropriate ways of expressing anger can go a long way in helping them react to situations. Some anger management programs focusing on cognitive behavior have been modified for adolescents and younger children. Three common types of cognitive behavioral therapy have been designed for youth, and they include life skills development, effective education, and problem-solving. Life skills focus on empathy, communication, assertiveness, etc. and they use modeling to teach reactions to anger.

Effective education pays attention to feelings of anger and relaxation. Problem-solving helps the patient to view the cause and effect of the situation instead of allowing anger to dominate. Some factor considered when selecting a therapy for children and adults include age, socialization, and severity of the anger challenge. For children, anger management therapy can be made more fun by including more engaging activities for them. Adolescents can gather more from the therapy sessions if they are helped in their natural social environment.

The anger management therapy selected for children and adolescent should have an intensity that matches the actions. For instance, if an adolescent has severe anger outbursts in class, he/she should have longer sessions with the school therapist. Some more severe anger reactions could call for tough actions such as management sessions in a juvenile correctional facility.

Individuals with Intellectual Disabilities

People with intellectual disabilities can have challenges with anger management. Depending on the individual and the environment, there are certain strategies used to minimize aggression from such people:

1. **Reactive strategies** are aimed at minimizing the impact of excessively aggressive behavior. A therapist

can use established protocols such as enforced isolation at the moment of anger.

2. **Contingency management** focuses on reshaping behavior through some forms of punishment and reinforcement.

3. **Ecological interventions** usually use the environment to bring on a calming effect on the angry person.

4. **Positive programming** normally teaches positive reaction skills in place of aggression.

Violent Criminals

Violent criminals are prone to anger because of their environment. Sometimes, imprisoning them makes it even worse because most of the incineration centers are uncontrolled. Normally, violent criminals need aggression in order to have their way. They, therefore, deploy anger to override the natural-rational human nature.

Substance Abusers

Alcohol and drug abusers are at a higher risk of getting angry and being unable to manage it. If an angry person cannot control certain aspects of his/her life well, the risk of anger rises.

Post-Traumatic Stress Disorder

Post-Traumatic stress disorder usually results in anger management challenges. People with brain injuries also have a challenge with anger management especially if the part of the brain responsible for impulse reactions is affected.

Chapter 3: Signs and Symptoms of Anger-Related Issues

Before one can learn the techniques to manage the emotion of anger, he/she need to learn the manifestations of anger. There is the need to answer questions such as: "What are the indications that I am angry? Which places, people, and events make me angry? What is my reaction when I feel angry? How do my actions affect others?" Getting the right answers to these questions takes time and attention. It is possible that a person will discover more than one thing that makes him/her angry. In the process, one will identify some of the signs that appear when anger sets in. These answers are usually the beginning of the anger management plan. They will help one to come up with a worthwhile plan that will help manage the anger.

Anger shows itself in different forms, and while some people are able to control the emotion, others are not. Some individuals have trouble taking control of their anger and some experience it outside the normal human scope. This anger that shows outside the normal emotion scope can present different types of disorders. Some of the widely accepted anger forms include chronic anger, overwhelming anger, passive anger, self-inflicted anger, volatile anger, and judgmental anger.

Chronic anger - This form of anger is long prolonged and normally has an impact on the immune system. It has also been linked to certain types of mental disorders.

Overwhelming anger – This is a form of anger that arises when life demands are too much for a person to cope with.

Passive anger - This form of anger does not always appear as anger and therefore can be hard to identify. Sometimes, the people experiencing passive anger do not even realize they are angry. In most cases, passive anger will be displayed as apathy, sarcasm, and meanness. A person experiencing passive anger will participate in self-defeating behavioral patterns such as alienating family and friends, skipping school and work, and performing poorly in social and professional situations. To outsiders, these self-sabotage patterns will appear as intentional although the affected person does not realize the cause and effect. Passive anger can be hard to recognize because it is often repressed. Counseling may help one to identify the emotion-triggering the self-sabotage activities and bring the underlying matters to light so that they can be dealt with.

Aggressive anger - The people that are prone to aggressive anger are normally aware of their feelings although they might not always understand the root cause of their behavior. In some cases, these people will redirect the anger outbursts towards scapegoats because they have difficulties with addressing the real challenge. Often, aggressive anger manifests itself as retaliatory or volatile anger and might lead to physical damages to people and property. Learning to identify the triggers and managing the symptoms is important in dealing with aggressive anger positively.

Chronic Anger

Basically, anger is an emotion designed to empower us to find constructive means of satisfying our needs and wants. However, people who have embraced chronical anger (long-term) end up getting disempowered. People with chronical anger view the world through a filter limited to their emotion. Those suffering from chronic anger have a deeply ingrained tendency that is reactive and hardly influenced by self-reflection and thought. Normally, these people have a narrowed vision, and their reactions are generally rigid. Consequently, there is a diminished power to their actions. The actions of the individuals normally sap the ability of the affected people to meet their wants and needs genuinely.

Chronic anger has many faces depending on the individual in question. For instance, some people will look to fight when intoxicated. A person will walk into a bar; pick someone to direct anger at and start a fight. Even if the person is stopped from fighting in the bar and kicked out, he/she will pick someone who is leaving the bar and keep fighting. Normally, this results in arrests or other tough consequences.

Chronic anger is also evident on the internet as people give predominantly selfish opinions. These statements made out of anger impair the capacity to be open, civil, compassionate and understanding. Chronic Anger is a cataract that clouds our judgment and vision. We are unable to see the good in others and even in ourselves. It makes us think that disagreements make us less human.

Chronic anger is in most cases pervasive and is evident in relationships, workplaces and other segments of life. It shows an ongoing vulnerability to becoming angry as well as a regular attitude of hostility. In most cases, chronic anger feeds from emotional and mental wounds and scars in people- The things that happened in the in our past, and we are unable to move past. These wounds tend to have originated from earlier physical and emotional neglect and abuse. They also might have originated from threats and losses in our recent lives. These losses can happen in employment, health, finances, social, economic status, etc.

While some people can clearly point at the source of their anger, others cannot associate their state with their former hurts and fears. The people who cannot link their current state with things that happened to them in the past are normally trying to deny their feelings or minimize the impact of looking at what they went through. Sometimes, the feeling of denial is due to shame and guilt. In most cases, they will blame themselves for the things that broke them in an attempt to hide from their confusion and anger regarding the events. Either way, the severity of the wounds incurred in the past may contribute to a state of hypersensitivity and over-reaction because very matter feels like maltreatment.

Many people who have been hurt in the past will embrace chronical pain as a mental armor with the intention of protecting self from suffering. This embrace can occur intentionally or unintentionally. Chronical anger can be used by a person to dodge self-reflection, something that is needed in order to create an identity. Anger helps one to avoid questions such as 'who am I and what is my purpose?'.

Without making such consideration, one will subscribe to the beliefs that he/she grew up with. Consequently, there will be no time to analyze the past and the current state of anger. Unless we have answers to questions that help us build our own character, we will still stick to chronic anger. We will not develop a complex personality that resonates with the person we are and want to be.

Chronic anger leaves us reactive, and we have a very weak personality and thus respond to every other drama in a drastic way. A lack of your own likes dislikes and desires leave you in a default state of reacting. A person can also avoid building a personality if he/she feels that the roles and duties placed upon him/her by parents or the society are unattainable. This stance is often evident in the attitude "I do not know who I am and want to be, but I'm sure I would not like to be you."

Other people embrace chronic anger in a bid to avoid taking responsibility for their lives. Generally, it is easier to blame another person or a circumstance for a certain situation rather than take responsibility. Blaming someone else helps one to renounce all the power and control which he/she might have used to alter the situation. Embracing chronic pain will help an individual to avoid looking for alternative courses of action even when in pain.

Holding onto anger is often supported by the need to protect self from being hurt again. Holding on to long-term anger helps us to develop a mindset of hyper-vigilance, that is, we are constantly on guard, waiting for someone to offend us. This mentality includes the wrongful belief that other people are looking for ways to harm us, or that we should not trust anyone. The mindset then hinders intimacy, and we are unable to invest and share at a deeper level emotionally. Again, the lack of trust adds to our quickness to avoid close relations and contributes to the inability to forgive ourselves and others.

By embracing pain, some people, are able to ward off the pain of mourning and grieving. They avoid identifying and accepting and pain behind the hurt, a process that is important for letting go of wounds. The inability to let go of what happened in the past leads to frozen time whereby one sees that he/she has limited opportunities and options to change things. Consequently, we are forced to focus on the past in a negative way that shades the perception of the future.

Whichever reason one chooses in order to embrace chronic anger, prolonged emotion can paralyze us. Chronic anger will promote a sense of disempowerment which will only lead to more anger in a bid to feel powerful. This prolonged anger may also contribute to alcohol and drug abuse and also self-loath. The people suffering from chronic anger will in most cases stick to blaming and hating others for their misery.

Chronic anger can also signify other disorders such as depression. It can also be as a result of other disorders. Just like depression, chronic anger also leads to pessimism towards the future. Consequently, a chronically angry person will not make a commitment to future goals that might even make life better. Chronic anger will make it hard for a person to envision the future without anger. One cannot even imagine a future that is bright, one full of happiness, fulfillment, and meaning.

One similarity between chronic anger and procrastination is that one feels protected. Procrastination protects one from the tension of engaging in an activity while chronic anger freezes a person in time, thus avoids the future. A chronically angry person will identify all sorts of excuses to avoid facing the future. For instance, instead of looking at the things influencing anger, he/she will explain that other people are not angry because they had it easy in life.

The identity of chronic anger is mostly from the hatred of other people who are different from us. Secondly, chronic anger rests on the belief that you cannot achieve happiness while those people you hate are still in your life. Their presence and existence feel like a hindrance. This rigid mentality gives other people too much power over our lives and at the same time robs us of every good thing.

When holding onto chronic anger, we fail to understand and realize the things we truly need. We can only identify our key desires when we pose and reflect on our anger and reactions. A close analysis will reveal the needs we have thwarted or threatened. It might be a desire for security, trust, respect, and safety. Note that holding onto that anger only makes it harder for one to meet the desires.

Sincerely speaking, life is difficult. In fact, life is neither fair nor just. Imagine a veteran who lost a limb while fighting for peace in the world. This veteran has every right to be angry and bitter. He/she can choose to stay in an abusive state, abuse drugs and rant about the failures of the government.

However, a good number of them choose to engage in constructive courses such as sports. They move forward with life in spite of their losses.

Holding onto anger only deprives you of a good life. Everybody has challenges, and the best option you have is to work through yours. Moving past challenges and hurts requires a strengthened will. Real change does not come easily; rather, it demands some serious actions in the face of pain. It does not matter if you get your motivation from faith, a bad or good memory, or a reward in the future. You have to put in a lot of will to break a habit. To let go of chronic anger, we need to be future focused on our behavior and thoughts.

It is important that we explore anger and the ways to manage it. Through counseling that includes deep self-reflection and practicing new skills, allowing space for mourning and grieving, and ultimately making peace with the past, one can find ways to make peace with the anger. Managing anger might require you to cultivate a voice of self-compassion that acknowledges personal pain and suffering.

Regardless of the person, we have become and the person we believe we are, there is a possibility that we can develop new habits. These habits will alter how we relate to our feelings, thoughts, and behavior in terms of anger. Anger management strategies will help us to lead a life the results in greater fulfillment.

Emotional Symptoms of Problems Related to Anger

One might think that the outburst of anger is the only indicator of an inability to deal with the emotion, but there are many symptoms that show unmanaged anger. Some of the other indicators showing that one is not dealing with anger in a healthy and effective way include constant irritability, anxiety, depression, sadness, resentment, rage, among others. A constant feeling of overwhelm, trouble with the organization of thoughts and feelings, and fantasies that one is better than others could also indicate an anger disorder or other anger issues.

Physical Symptoms of Problems Related to Anger

There are physical indicators of anger, for instance, heart palpitation, tingles, increased blood pressure, fatigue, headaches, clenched jaws, grinding teeth, stomach ache, headache, dizziness, trembling and shaking, sweating, feeling hot in the face, and pressure in the head.

Other symptoms that might indicate a failure in anger management include: beginning to yell and raise voice on matters that are small, getting sarcastic, raising the voice, screaming and crying, losing one's sense of humor, acting abusively, etc.

Chapter 4: The Costs of Anger

Anger has both psychological and physiological processes and consequences. As such, anger can have a negative impact on the physical and emotional state of health. The negative relationship between anger and heart diseases has proven to be true.

Health Costs

Blood Pressure and Heart Disease

Scientists have found that there is a direct connection between the state of being constantly competitive, aggressive, and angry, and early heart disease. For instance, recent studies show that men who lack anger management skills tend to have higher chances of suffering from heart disease before they reach the age of 55 compared to their peers. Another study revealed that it is easier to accurately predict the likelihood of getting a heart attack for men using their hostility rating. Hostility rating refers to how irritable and hostile one is towards the other. It is easier to predict a heart attack through anger rating than it is with other causes such as cholesterol levels, tobacco smoking, alcohol intake etc.

The expression of hostility and anger also relate to blood pressure reactivity and hypertension (high blood pressure). In a study that analyzed the effects of distraction and harassment on men trying to perform a task, only the men who were highly hostile showed increased blood pressure levels and higher blood flow rates into the muscles. The men with lower scores on the scale of hostility rating did not show the above mentioned physiological changes. The men with higher hostility levels also reported a more lingering irritation and anger than those with lower levels. The evidence from these studies and other similar ones revealed that there is a high link between proneness to physiological hyperactivity and anger. Some people tend to become easily aroused sand they stay stressed for longer periods thus bringing about cumulative and significant damages to their bodies.

Numerous studies have clearly revealed that; having constant chronic hostility, aggression, and anger will raise your chance of developing an array of deadly heart diseases y five times the normal rate. The more hostile you are, the higher the risk of heart disease. If you find that you lose your temper whenever you have to wait for long in the line in a grocery store, or if the traffic jam gets you really mad, it is important that you check the damage you might be bringing upon yourself. Anger can slowly destroy your life or even kill you.

Personality Types and Anger

There are different types of personality classified according to unique characteristics. The chronically hostile, irritable, and angry people are normally found under the personality 'type A.' The people with personalities that are more laid back are classified as 'type B.' These classifications were invented by doctors Meyer Friedman and Ray Rosenman in the late 1950s as a means of differentiating between the patients that have higher chances of having heart diseases and those with low chances. 'Type A' personalities are more likely to achieve great success professionally, but they tend to display more aggression and competitive personality traits.

The type B personality tends to approach life through an easygoing route. Consequently, the 'type A' personalities are more prone to heart attacks than 'type B.' To be specific, 'type A' personalities show the following traits; quick to anger, competitiveness, explosive reactivity, irritability, impatience, and hostility. These traits indicate a high probability of heart disease.

On the brighter side, the personality 'type A' people are often very determined and driven to succeed. They do not allow anything to stand in their way when they are pursuing their goals. They are focused, and consequently, they are always in a hurry. These people lack patience for their colleagues and people around them especially those in the 'type B' personality. The type A personalities seem like they are ignoring others mostly because their mind is occupied by other things or they are busy with something else. These people also tend to be very judgmental and criticize a lot of things. They often focus on the weaknesses of other people, concentrating on matters lateness, indifference, poor driving skills, etc. The 'type A' personality people tend to become angry at those they deem incompetent or having some shortcomings.

Physiologically, men in the 'type A' personality category (more so those with high hostility levels) show a lower parasympathetic nervous system response compared to those with a more laid back personality type B. The parasympathetic nervous system refers to the part of the nervous system that is responsible for calming down during moments of anger. The sympathetic nervous system (or SNS) is the opposite of the parasympathetic nervous system which brings about arousal during moments of anger. The Sympathetic nervous system is responsible for flooding the body with stress hormones that cause arousal. These stress hormones include adrenaline and noradrenaline primarily. The parasympathetic nervous system plays the role of countering the arousal hormones by releasing acetylcholine which neutralizes the other hormones, allowing the body to relax and calm down. When a healthy parasympathetic nervous system responds, it causes the body to work less hard therefore reducing the strain placed on organs such as the heart and veins. However, because the parasympathetic nervous system of 'type A' men is weaker than normal, they are normally unable to calm down and therefore suffer bodily damage.

Strangely, even the immune system of the people with type A personality seems to be weaker. The immune system plays a big role in helping the body to keep free of cancer cells by producing other killer cells that are responsible for killing tumor cells once they form in the body. One study revealed that the students with high hostility rates (Type A) had fewer killer cells in the body during periods of high stress such as when taking difficult exams. This was not the case for Type B personality students.

Summarily, unlike the mellow type B personality, type A people are wired differently in that, they spend more time while influenced by an aroused nervous system. This does not happen to personality type B. The repeated arousal of blood pressure and heart rate, and other varieties of factors involved in the arousal response of type A causes cumulative and to some extent non-repairable damage to the organs and tissues in the body. The differences in stress exposure account for the higher early death rates associated with the type A personality category.

Social Costs

Anger does not only have physical effects; rather, it also accounts for a number of emotional and social costs. Anger correlates with hostility which in turn makes it hard for people to have health and constructive relationship. Because of the constant nature of anger, hostile people will keep losing friends and retaining very few close relationships. Additionally, hostile people are more likely to suffer from depression and have a higher probability of being abusive towards others both physically and verbally. Most importantly, chronic anger interferes with the intimacy in a personal relationship whether it is with a family member or a partner. It is hard for normal people to relax their guard when dealing with an angry person; therefore, the strained relationships.

At first glance, this loss of relationships may not sound like a bad fate especially for those who like their space. However, researches show that it is important for one to have healthy and supportive relationships with friends, family, colleagues, and coworkers in order to maintain health. Having the social support of peers helps one to keep off emotional problems and deep-seated health conditions such as heart diseases. People are less likely to suffer from debilitating depression if they have strong and viable social support.

Angry people tend to have a cynical attitude towards others and will often fail to utilize help when it is availed to them. These people also fail to recognize the impact of their actions and behavior on others; they hardly realize that they are pushing people away gradually. Anger makes these people ridicule genuine help from friends. Anger has also been linked to bad eating and drinking habits and also substance abuse. Because angry people do not keep links with other people, there will be no one to help them deal with bad habits—thus increasing the chances of serious health consequences.

The physiological response and arousal due to anger evolved so that people can handle physical threats constructively. However, in the world of today, there are very few occasions that need one to respond with physical aggression. When you look at workplaces, social gatherings, homes, schools, etc., there are very few instances where physical fights and verbal altercations are viable. Attacking a boss will lead to loss of the job and fighting a slow motorist on the highway will actually land you in court.

Unmanaged anger will lead you to the courts, make you lose your job, and even get secluded by family and friends. The people suffering from uncontrolled anger will not only suffer physically but also socially and emotionally. It is important that one gets a grip on any aggressive and disruptive behavior arising from mismanaged anger.

Motivational Costs and Effects of Anger

As seen earlier, anger does not affect the physical state of a person only. It also affects the psychological state of a person. Have you ever wondered why it is hard for angry people just to let go of their habits? There are some beliefs and motivational benefits linked to anger. Some of these benefits are short-sighted; others are healthy, while others are self-destructive.

On the bright side, anger tends to generate a feeling of control and power in a situation that would otherwise involve fear and feeling weak. Before the feeling of anger, one might lack the sense of strength, but as the emotion rises, the control and righteousness motivate the person to change and challenge the difficult social or interpersonal injustice. When anger is handled appropriately, it will help one to motivate others in winning a case that would otherwise be impossible to handle. Sometimes, anger gives one a rest from the feeling of fear and vulnerability; it is a good way of venting frustrations and tensions.

Anger increases the energy necessary to defend one when a wrong is being perpetrated. For instance, if one is a victim of domestic violence for a long time, and the anger gets to a boiling point, the vulnerability disappears, and strength takes over helping the person to leave the abusive relationship. In such scenarios, anger can be a very positive force in life. It helps one to carry on and persevere when fighting for a good cause, for instance, Mahatma Gandhi and other freedom fighters.

Though anger has positive motivations, it also has negative ones. Anger is capable of creating and reinforcing a false feeling of entitlement, that is, an illusory feeling of superiority that enables one to justify immoral acts. For example, aggression that is motivated by anger can be used to justify terrorism or to bully and coerce people into doing the things one wants even if it is against their will. Angry people are more likely to subscribe to the philosophy that the end justifies the means and then select some unjustified means of achieving their goals. If anger has led you to the dark side in any way such as it led Eric Harris and Dylan Klebold the school shooters who murdered their fellow students in Colorado in 1999, then it is time to seek for help.

There is a need to realize that anger can have either a positive or negative effect. If therefore, anger gets to a boiling point and makes you walk away from an abusive spouse, then that anger is good. But if you use the anger to intimidate and frighten others to doing what you want even without considering the consequences, then there is a danger, and you are acting as badly as a bully.

Chapter 5: Anger and Mental Health

Anger is not always a disorder by itself. Sometimes, it can signify another mental disorder. When assessing anger, a therapist should address any underlying diagnosis. There are a number of mental conditions closely linked to anger, including:

- **Bipolar disorder** - One common feature of mania is irritability. A person may have anger symptoms in the depressive phase.
- **Major depression** - Anger may be directed at self or others.
- **Narcissistic personality disorder** - A narcissistic person may lash out in anger if someone hurts or attacks his/her ego. They use anger to mask other feelings such as fear and inferiority.
- **Oppositional defiant behavior** - Hostile or angry behavior is one of the major signs of ODD in children.
- **Post-traumatic stress disorder** - PTSD often leads to an outburst of anger even without provocation. The stress pushes a person to the edge such that the mind stops functioning normally.

The Connection Between Anger and Stress

You might ask yourself if stress is the same as anger. Is stress a result of anger or is anger a result of stress? People say that there is more anger in the world today than 20 years ago. Considering the current living conditions, this might be true. Other people say that there is more anger today and it is evident in workplace violence, road rage, school shootouts, etc. Stress can increase certain problems and if you experience anger often, chances are, stress will make it worse.

Healthy stress is very good when controlled. Eustress (Healthy stress) makes us get out of bed in the morning and pursue our dreams. It is also the thing that makes us stay attentive throughout the day. This type of stress does not lead to irritability or anger. The people lacking Eustress are normally referred to as unmotivated or lazy by others.
On the other hand, there is a form of stress called distress. This type of stress makes people irritable or downright angry. This stress often happens when anger is too much and no longer acting as a motivator. Stress can be overwhelming when a combination of stressors piles up on a person. One day, the stress becomes too much, and the person does not know how to handle it thus bursts out in anger.

Is there another feeling that is behind stress and anger? When one is feeling angry or stress there are other feelings powering it. In most cases, one gets stressed or angry when he/she feels helpless, disrespected, overwhelmed, fearful etc. It is important to look at the feelings behind the stress and anger in order to identify the most viable treatment. Understanding the cause of your action helps you to select steps that will help you relax.

Once you have identified the thoughts and feelings contributing to anger and stress, look at the environment surrounding you. Is your environment chaotic? Is your home or work environment making you feel too fatigued and irritable? Once you see the environmental stressors find ways to avoid or deal with them. Sometimes the solutions are limited to changing your mentality

There are substances that can increase anger and stress, including sugar, caffeine, nicotine, and excess food. There are also substances and practices that can help to reduce stress including exercises, learning communication, hobbies, journaling, yoga, deep breathing, Qigong, and engaging in social activities.

Quick Tips for Managing Stress and Anger

- Ask yourself, "Will it matter tomorrow, next week, or next month?"
- Understand that the only person responsible for you is yourself.
- Understand that anger and stress is energy. It is up to you to decide the way you want to use it—positively or negatively.
- Understand that if you allow other people to stress you, you are giving them the power to control you. Do you really want other people to manage your feelings?

The Impact of Anger and Stress

Ideally, we should be in a state of homeostasis - balanced feeling and living. Physically everything should be working perfectly and so should the emotions. There should be a full state of wellbeing, with no stress, anguish or anger. However, many things happen, upsetting that balance thus sending us into other states of existence. The dangers of the outside world are the leading cause of imbalances. An author and blogger called Robert M. Sapolsky, MD states that zebras do not get ulcers. In his book called "Why, Zebras Don't Get Ulcers," D r. Sapolsky, states that when a zebra gets threatened by a predator, its alert senses rise. The blood pressure increases, adrenaline flow intensifies, and the animal gets into the fight or flight mode. Blood rushes to the legs and the heart; thus the zebra runs very fast. The zebra will either escape or die but either way, it forgets as soon as the situation has ended. However, that does not apply to humans.

With us, stress and anger will last long after the situation is over. Generally, humans are designed to ruminate on things and find solutions. The rumination on the dangerous or maddening situation results in increased levels of blood pressure and adrenaline. In fact, we will be in a state where we can sense anger when there is none. That reaction tells you why you might get angry at a traffic jam. The problem is, such high levels of alertness due to stress and anger are harmful to health. We should learn ways to manage stress and anger, and like the zebra, get back to the state of equilibrium.

Anger and Your Beliefs

As we have seen, there are a variety of reasons why one can get angry. Did you know or even suspect that the belief system of a person can cause a whole bout of anger? Researchers have found that a person's beliefs affect their anger levels.

What do you believe in? Which beliefs do you hold dear? Which ones do you have yet they no longer serve you? Which ones are bringing you harm? By definition, a belief is something that you take as truth and thus hold onto it. It can be a list of dos and don'ts—a values system. For instance, you can believe that being a good person will get through life, you will always get your way, everyone should be kind at all circumstances, and that no one will take advantage of you. How true is that belief?

Many beliefs are formed during childhood based on what one is taught or what he/she has observed. The beliefs are often instilled by parents, guardians, teachers, or other authority figures. In many cases, these teachings are an asset when used well. However, some of them become beliefs that result in problems later in life. For instance, the people who are lead to believe that they should always have their way are substantially angrier than those who were taught that they could not win all the time.

The next time you feel upset; take a close look at the things you believe in. Are they contributing to your anger? Are they rational? Many times, a belief that leads to anger is irrational or impractical. Once you identify the specific problem with the belief, adjust it. For instance, you may realize that a certain belief makes it hard for you to stay calm and rational. It is better to let it go of the absurd beliefs than to remain angry.

Another adjustment that you can make is adding understanding to your belief. For instance, if you believe that everyone should treat you fairly every other time, you should adjust to "I should be treated right, but there are times when I will be treated unfairly." That is life. Learn how to roll with it rather than taking it head-on.

You might want to insist that your beliefs are right and rational. Testing your beliefs will help you learn if your anger is justified. Remember, anger is beneficial when used properly. For instance, the people who use anger to stand up for themselves are using it in the right way. Anger can help you escape from situations where someone mistreats you. Were it not for the people who used anger in a justified way, we would not have some civil rights, some people would still be excluded from voting, and there would be a lot of injustices in the world. When anger is justified, use the energy in a positive way. Avoid violence. Do not be verbally abusive. Avoid things that would hurt someone else.

The Iceberg

Anger is what we normally see. When a person is angry, we can see the signs, the physical changes inform us. Some people will sweat, others will clench fists and others will raise their voices. When you check closely, anger is actually the iceberg. What we all see is just the tip. There is a complex feeling behind the symptomatic, and it varies from one person to the other. The real iceberg can be made up of insecurities, fear, hurt pride, and frustration, feeling disrespected and other emotions.

Because the anger we see is just the iceberg, it takes some through detective work to identify the real cause. One has to identify the underlying issue, in order to help the angry person. The first step to controlling anger is to ask yourself, "what is causing these emotions?" "What makes me feel this way?" When a person examines the feelings and the causes of anger, then he/she can address the problem. Basic techniques such as breathing, counting, and meditating will help you deal with the tip of the iceberg in the short term, but more will be required for long term solutions.

Understanding the iceberg is a great way to control your own anger and that of other people. When you use the iceberg theory to analyze anger, it will be easy for you to understand the anger of another person. For instance, when a coworker is getting angry at work because of a reason that is minute, you will be able to see that there is another thing behind the current emotion. It is hard for you to reciprocate anger with anger when you know that they are acting out of fear, jealousy, insecurity, hurt, or past things. When we understand this, it is easier to be gentle in our reactions and empathic.

Consequently, we will be able to help the person to deal with anger or at least stay calm. It is sad that many people and more so men believe that it is okay to show anger through aggression and violence while it is wrong to show other emotions such as sadness, fear, guilt or inferiority. Most of the feelings that lead to loss of control are part of the anger iceberg. These feelings one is not allowed to show are part of the triggers of anger hidden beneath the surface. As such, one should look at all the feelings fueling the anger. Instead of taking the macho route and expressing what is socially acceptable, look for ways to discuss your true feelings. Look past the anger and deal with the real problems, it will help you deal with your own emotions as well as those of the people around you.

Anger, Alcohol, and Drug Abuse

Remember that the anger we see in people and in ourselves is just the tip of the iceberg. There is more to it. Some people will have anger management issues stemming from drug and substance abuse. Others have anger issues because of brain damage.

In events where a person is abusing drugs and has anger management issues, the main problem is that the drugs are attacking the functionality of the brain. The more one uses drugs, the angrier he/she become. A variety of reasons can contribute to such anger. For instance, when the person runs out of drugs, he/she will get angry. If there are family or personal issues arising due to the drugs, and the affected person is unable to manage them, he/she will be angry. Direct chemical attacks on the brain can result in anger.

Note that it is usually difficult to manage anger if the angry person uses drugs frequently. A therapist can work with such a person until he/she runs out of breath and it will probably not work. Such people need help with substance abuse before they can work on anger. A substance abuse program will help the patient more than a direct anger management program.

Some people have anger problems because of brain injuries. The sections of the brain responsible for controlling anger and other impulses are referred to as frontal lobes, and they are located right behind the forehead. An accident such as a car crash, hitting your head or falling can turn an otherwise calm person into an enraged and angry individual. Actually, it is very easy to damage the brain to the extent where you keep losing your temper. In the event that an angry person once had an accident that might have damaged the brain, it is advisable for him/her to visit a neurologist before engaging an anger management therapist. There are medical interventions for some of these cases. They help a person before he/she can go for therapy. Most of the cases involving brain injury require one to combine psychiatric drugs with anger management programs. Although many people believe there is no hope for people with anger issues resulting from brain injuries, there is some help. A large number of people have learned to manage anger in spite of injuries. However, it takes a lot of dedication and work.

Chapter 6: The Choice to Manage Anger

Anger management is often described as the ability to deploy anger successfully. The best-fitted goal of anger management involves regulating and controlling anger so that it does not cause problems. Although anger is a part of human emotions, the ways we choose to express it may not be acceptable or normal to the people and around us. Once a person suspects that he/she has anger problems, or if the trustable people around you tell you that you have challenges with managing your anger, there is the need to learn about how to have better control over the emotion.

There is a variety of anger management programs and information available for each person through different platforms. These programs and plans are designed to help one to manage anger and to develop a healthy emotional life. Good anger helps one to maintain a good relationship with other people and as such, anger management programs will help you to master your anger problem. However, just like any other programs, the ones designed for anger management will benefit the people that follow them fully and apply all they have to offer.

Learning how to control anger requires one to make a deep commitment because it is an ongoing task. It requires a lot of changes from the past ways. You will be required to reconsider the automatic responses used formally. You will also be required to take more responsibility for actions and thoughts that did not require much thought in the past. All of the above changes will require a plan and a lot of discipline. In an effort to assist you in gaining this plan and discipline, we will help you to review the ways through which normal people approach large changes. This perspective will help you in the anger management process. It is important to understand the best way to approach a challenge just as it is important to overcome the problem.

The Stages of Change

Normally, people go through a particular predictable set of stages as they work through life-changing events. The progress through the stages is to a large extent accredited to a combination of technique, motivation, and dedication. Some individuals move at a fast pace through the stages while others take their time and in some cases, they take a step or two backward before they can move forward again.

As you study the following stages, it is important to consider how each stage affected your life during a time of change. How did the stages play out in your life? It is also good to consider how you will work through the challenges met at each stage as you pursue your anger management goals. There is no rule stating that one must follow the sequence of the stages as listed below but one should ensure that he/she understands each stage well in order to achieve the set goals.

The decision to control anger will definitely present a big change in the way one lives his/her life. It is hard for one to want to make a big change in life unless there is a big thing that comes along and makes him/her reconsider the old ways of doing things. There are things that appear in the life of an individual motivating them to seek new ways of handling matter. Majority of people only make changes when they have experienced serious consequences of anger in their personal, occupational, and social lives. One may seek help after a spouse has filed for a divorce after a big fight or has lost a job due to workplace disagreement. Some people will look for help when they realize by themselves that they are holding too much anger while others will seek help just to get other people off their back.

Awareness stage: The awareness stage normally begins when the angry person seeks information on anger management such as what is anger; how does it affect relationships and health? How can it be controlled?

Preparation stage: The difference between the awareness stage and preparation stage is commitment. In the awareness stage, the person concentrates on gathering information. On the other hand, the preparation stage involves the decision to express anger in a constructive way. Besides commitment, preparation also involves planning and self-study. During all stages and more so the preparation stage, it is important for one to keep an anger management journal where he/she records the things making him/ her angry, the feelings and reactions, and the consequences. The anger journal helps one to become more aware of and to identify the triggers of anger and thus to give an insight into the proportions of anger. The more you study your anger, the higher the chances of changing the way you express it.

Action stage: This stage involves the initiation of real change. One may decide to take a professional course on anger management or to buy a set of guideline books, recordings, or videos. Action stage also involves designing a personal program to help you on an individual basis. However, regardless of the program one uses, it will not be of any help if the person does not apply them with persistence and dedication.

Maintaining gains: The maintenance stage of life changes is a never-ending stage. It involves the realization and acceptance that you are human and are prone to mistakes, you are not perfect, and at times, you will act inappropriately, but the best part, you can always recover from the behavior lapses. Reaching a sustained behavior change takes time. In some cases, it will take multiple failures and attempts before one can achieve the set goal. Every time one lapses into old behavior, he/she uses the strategies and tools he/she has learned along the way to get back from where they fell.

It is particularly hard for the majority of the people with anger problems to gather the motivation necessary for a serious commitment to work through an anger management program. You see, the anger has a self-justifying and seductive quality to itself; therefore, people will typically not be drawn to anger management by their own will. Most of the cases will involve serious the person suffering serious consequences of the anger before the realization that there is a need for help in controlling the outbursts. Even after the realization, the motivation for sticking to the program can be really slim.

Normally, angry people will quit attending an anger management program just before they finish it and in other cases, those who finish might not apply the techniques they learned. As such, most people require a repetition of anger management programs for a number of times before they can truly understand the message they need to incorporate in their lives on their own.

Mandatory Anger Management Treatment

As seen earlier, not all people will willingly look for help when they have anger management issues. Remember that anger has motivations; things that make it feel good. However, in extreme cases, the court can mandate people to attend anger treatment programs. If one is causing harm to others through anger, and he/she demonstrates the unwillingness to work on the habits, the court is willing to require him/her to attend the classes. An employer can also mandate an angry employee to attend anger management seminars and programs even though it is through the sponsorship of employee assistance programs.

In the event that you have been mandated by a court or employer to attend anger management treatment programs, it is vital that you make the best out of the demand. Better participate fully in the program. It might not be your will to go through the program, but please understand that it is for your good. The people who have mandated you have good intentions; they want you to have control of your life before other people start controlling it for you. They are trying to protect you from losing your job, losing your relationships and even going to jail. Learning the ways through which you can apply anger in a more productive way will improve your life and reduce the chances of suffering from certain diseases and premature deaths. Keeping this realization in mind will help you participate fully and benefit from the anger management program.

Commitment is essential if you want actually to get the full benefits of the program. Learn and practice the techniques many times to help you change your behavior. The only ticket that guarantees success in an anger management program is to do what it takes to ensure that the program works. Remember that there might be negative effects if you fail to follow the entire program. Real change will only occur if you cooperate. Without full cooperation, even a genuine opportunity to change lives will not help you.

Why You Have to Stay Cool

In most cases, anger comes with a lot of justification: you feel right, and the other person is wrong. However, as seen earlier, you cannot go around blowing the anger on every other person; even the social norms do not allow that. It is not okay to go attacking other people just because you feel they are targets. There are many consequences of unrestrained anger, and the punishments that might be given can be devastating. In the world of today where people are terrorized, violent outbursts are not well accepted; therefore, if you attack someone physically, regardless of the reasons, there is a good chance you will be arrested or punished. At work, if you attack a customer, a coworker or even the boss, there are high chances that you will be fired from the job. If the attack lands on your child, be sure that he/she will be taken from your custody. If the child is not taken away, then be sure you have taught him/her that it is okay to go about busting with anger towards others. If you bust at your friends, chances are they will walk away from you and refrain from helping you.

When you consider all the risks linked to unmanaged anger, it is important to develop a list of the reasons why you should stay cool and calm in certain situations. Read over the reasons often so that they can stay clear and fixed in your head. The reasons you choose should be based on practical consequences that might fall on you if you allow yourself to get out of control.

Some examples of the reasons you can write down include:
- "I should stay calm so as to retain my job."
- "I should stay calm, so I avoid getting arrested."
- "I need to remain calm, so my children will not learn bad anger habits from me."
- "I need to stay calm, so my spouse will not leave me, etc."

The Major Challenges Hindering the Cultivation of Healthy Anger

Many people with destructive anger look for ways to overcome it either on their own accord or because someone, for instance, a spouse has asked them to. Once a person realizes and acknowledges the effect of destructive anger, he/she seeks for ways and strategies to minimize the reactivity and vulnerability to anger. However, these people often fail in their anger management attempts.

They may be strongly motivated to make the required changes, but conflicting mentalities undermine the efforts. Holding and showing anger serves a purpose. For instance, anger may become an emotional armor helping in distracting and protecting the individual from consciously enduring the specific threat. Such anger leads to a form of peace that consoles the affected person. As such, the affected person will have a conflict when making the necessary changes for anger management.

In order to overcome the challenges that undermine the cultivation of healthy anger, one must recognize and overcome them. Some of these challenges include:

1. **The underestimation of the work that it will take to change**

    We are living in a society that believes in quick fixes for everything. Many things are now solved easily using advanced technology. You warm your food in a few seconds, get to the store in a few minutes, and even enjoy instant showers. However, quick fixes cannot apply to practices developed over many years. The cultivation of healthy anger needs time, patience and commitment.

2. **Anger towards the amount of effort needed for change**

    After realizing that good anger will only develop out of commitment, dedication, and patience, many people feel angrier. This anger might even lead to resentment towards the people that lack such anger challenges.

3. **Anger normally works in the short-term.**

   The fact that anger is only a short term solution to challenges makes the affected person feel lonely and isolated. Anger acts as a distraction from threatening feelings and inner pain. In other cases, anger can be used to invoke anxiety and fear in other people thus giving a feeling of power to the angry person. Once the anger is gone, the person will feel isolated, and as such, he/she might not be willing to do all it takes to cultivate healthy anger.

4. **Discomfort in reflection**

   In order to understand oneself, there is a need for solitude and reflection. Taking time to reflect allows us to become more mindful of how we facilitate our anger. However, the majority of people find reflection and solitude extremely uncomfortable. Normally, society demands that we should be social and avoid self-indulgence.

5. **Thinking and feeling that one needs to change habits are two different things.**

   A person may think that he/she needs to change the habits but lack the will power. However, when there is the feeling that one needs to change his/her habits, and then he/she is likely to pursue the needed changes. It might be challenging to develop healthy anger when the mind and the heart are disagreeing.

6. **Familiarity**

   Years of living with certain characteristics make us familiar and comfortable with the person we become. For instance, when one lives with anger for too long, he/she might start thinking that anger is a normal part of their lives. We become comfortable with ourselves because we have lived in a particular way for many years.

   The truth is, we are subject to change and are very much dependent on the array of habits we develop and follow over the years. Consequently, we can cultivate better and more helpful ways to deal with life just as we learned the ways we are familiar with.

7. **The tension that accompanies applying new skills**

   We all know the feeling that accompanies the learning of new skills. When we are trying out new things, we are afraid that we might fail- unsure of the unknown. There is a feeling of awkwardness, inadequacy, intolerance, and some degree of self-doubt. Acquiring new skills calls for a strong frustration tolerance rate. Moments of learning and applying new skills call for self-love and compassion. They call for the realization that mistakes are a normal part of life. It is therefore important that we set realistic goals when developing healthy anger; otherwise, we might feel frustrated and give up.

8. **The rewarding feeling that accompanies anger**

   In some cases, anger is accompanied by a physical rush that erases thoughts of doubt and makes one feel energized and alive. Anger makes the level of cortisol hormone to increase. This hormone helps people to respond to stressful situations thus the increased feeling of energy. Unfortunately, the physical rush hinders the capacity to make a sound judgment. One essential ingredient of healthy anger is the ability to be mindful of the rush rather than acting out of it. This mindfulness involves identifying the things that are in our best interest in the long term.

9. **Using anger to avoid responsibility**

   Some people use anger to avoid responsibility. There are hundreds of people who hold onto anger and blame someone else for their fate. These people may blame their parents, relatives, employers, coworkers etc., who they believe is responsible for their suffering. Even long after the accused people are gone, those holding onto such anger continue to blame them. In a way, this anger reflects a particular degree of dependency. Contradictorily, letting go of this anger involves letting go of blame and accepting responsibility for the role we played. Healthy anger involves realizing that it is upon us to find the meaning and structure of our lives and to also take the steps towards living our best.

10. **Concentrating on the activities that are rewarding in the short term**

    Many of the activities that the people want to pursue in an effort to develop healthy anger are short term and give results for a very short frame of time. However, it takes a lot of self-reflection to achieve healthy anger. We often look for fun-filled activities that divert our attention in the short run rather than the long term activities that that may potentially lead to a more lasting and deeper gratification. Committing to healthy anger requires one to concentrate on the long-term benefits and thus look for lasting anger management methods.

11. **Mental disorders**

    There are certain types of mental disorders that undermine the commitment and motivation for change concerning anger. A mental disorder may require treatment before a person starts cultivating healthy habits in any direction. These may call for psychotherapy and or medication.

Some of the strategies that one may use to deal with these challenges include:

1. Identify the obstacles that might affect the quest for healthy anger. Spotting the main hindrances of healthy anger will help one to mitigate them.

2. Write a list of reasons why you need to cultivate healthy anger, the importance, the intended

achievement, and the differences you hope to see in your life.

3. Identify a specific time in your daily schedule where you practice the activities helping in developing healthy anger.

4. Keep track of the main challenges blocking your achievement and identify where you might fail.

5. Seek help from other people that might help you achieve your goals for instance family and professionals.

6. Engage in formal and informal meditation activities. They will help you to gain further awareness of the challenges to progress.

7. Savor and celebrate the moments of progress. Every sight change should be appreciated because it is a sign of positive progress.

Chapter 7: Steps to Managing Anger Effectively

Using an Anger Diary

One of the most recommended techniques for dealing with anger includes using an anger diary or journal. This diary comes in handy after a person has identified the anger ratings.

Anger rating refers to a technique applied by people to measure the levels of anger. Keeping in mind the fact that anger is not a physical state that can be measured like body temperature using a physical gadget, one has to identify a personal scale with ratings. Anger is complex because it involves physical, emotional, and psychological aspects; therefore, it can be hard to rate.

One should picture a form of thermometer that measures the degree of anger that he/she is feeling at any one given time. When you start feeling irritated or frustrated, the mercury in the thermometer begins to rise, when angry but in control, the mercury rises halfway, and when not in control, the thermometer reads maximum. One can rate the anger from 0 to 100 whereby zero means one is in control while 100 signifies full rage.

Anger ratings are essential because they give one feedback about the likelihood of losing control or exploding at any given moment. By learning to tract anger, one will recognize the moments of challenge, the chances of losing and maintaining control, and the steps to take in order to calm down.

Although anger ratings help one to become conscious of the anger levels, it does not enable him/her to stop being angry. As such, one needs to develop a plan to help calm down and manage anger. Some of the things that one might incorporate in the plan are to 'take time out' when anger starts to set in, that is, to move away from the person or thing that is making one lose the calm. Another means of dealing with anger may include changing the conversation from the topic that is irritating to that which is more neutral.

There are many aspects that one may apply to diffuse a situation that invokes anger. The best techniques include those that help one to keep calm without damaging pride. Because each person has unique strengths and weaknesses, the list of strategies and plan should be customized to meet the specific needs.

As the saying goes, "Prevention is the best medicine." It is important to be able to predict the situations that might provoke anger. This ability will tremendously help a person to control and keep the temper under control. One may choose to avoid provoking situations completely, and if avoidance is not possible, then one will be able to prepare with ways to mitigate the danger of losing control before entering the dangerous situation.

An anger journal or diary can be a very useful tool to help you keep a record of experiences with anger. In the dairy, one should make daily recordings of the provocative situations encountered. In order to reap the maximum benefits from the diary, there are certain types of information that one needs to record for every provocative event:

- In the situation, which part was provocative?
- Which particular part made you feel pained or stressed?
- What thoughts were running through your head during the situation?
- Referring to the anger rating, how angry did you feel?
- How did you behave?
- What was the effect of your behavior on yourself and others?
- What exactly happened?
- How did your body react?
- Did your head hurt?
- Did you fight or fright?
- Did you scream, slam doors, or become sarcastic?
- What were the consequences of the situation?

After recording this information for a period of time, review the diary and identify the reoccurring themes, the constants triggers, the things that make you lose your calm. The triggers can fall under certain categories including:

- People failing to do what is expected of them or doing what is not expected
- Situational events for instance traffic jams, ringing phones, computer problems, etc.
- People taking advantage of others
- Anger and disappointment by self
- A combination of any of the above categories

During the review of the diary, it is also important for one to look for thoughts that trigger anger. These thoughts will be identifiable because they tend to reoccur and will most probably involve some of these themes:

- The thought that those who offended you did it intentionally cause harm
- The perception that you have been harmed and victimized
- The belief that the other persons were wrong and that they should have acted in a different way.
- The thought that those who harmed you are stupid and evil

The diary will also help you to identify the instances where you felt harmed and the reasons as to why you felt that way. Why do you think the person did a deliberate thing to harm you and why do you think the person was wrong and you were right? Tracking these thoughts will help a person start seeing the common aspects of these experiences. Some types of trigger thoughts include:

- People do not care about you; they are not paying enough attention to your needs
- People expect and demand too much from you
- Other people are inconsiderate and rude
- Others are selfish and are taking advantage of you
- Others think of only themselves and use people
- People shame, criticize and disrespect you
- People are mean or cruel, stupid and incompetent, thoughtless and irresponsible, etc.

- People look for ways to push you further down and do not offer assistance
- Majority of people are lazy and will do anything to avoid their share of work
- People are trying to manipulate or control you
- People are slowing you down

There are certain situations when these themes are more likely to occur including:

- When someone says no
- When expressing and receiving negative feelings
- When dealing with a situation where there is no cooperation
- When speaking about things that annoy you
- When protesting,
- When proposing and opposing an idea

At the bottom of every trigger thought there is a notion that people are behaving improperly and that you have the right to be angry with them. Most people will identify a number of thoughts that trigger anger. You should look for instances and situations that lead to anger and see if you can identify the triggering thoughts that led to the anger.

The purpose of the diary is to help one to identify the behavioral patterns and recurring specifications that really make one lose calm. When used well, the diary enables one to observe behaviors and feelings accurately. Consequently, one will be able to spot the mitigation plans to help manage anger. When one understands the ways through which he/she feels anger, he/she is able to plan strategies to deal with the anger more productively.

Once you have identified the triggers, the need to deactivate them arises.

Identifying and understanding anger triggers and their theme helps one to work more constructively. Remember that anger triggering thoughts occur on their own; therefore; one will be required to work consciously in order to substitute the anger with something more positive.

For instance, if you are driving on a freeway, then something obstructs you, take conscious note of the physiological signs of anger that indicate an upset. Next, take a deep breath and look into the situation more rationally instead of following the impulse to attack. It is important to look at the situation rationally instead of assuming that the obstruction was deliberate (which might be the first thought in situations of anger). Identifying that the provoking action was not deliberately directed at you will go a long way in helping you deal with anger rationally with more tolerance.

When you feel that your anger is justified, you only create room for more anger even when it does not make sense. It will be better if you stop justifying anger soon in order to help it recede faster. While all anger might be legitimate and at the moment of feeling it, that does not justify any negative acts done out of anger. Keep in mind that excessive uncontrolled anger is bad for health and it causes destructions towards the important relationships with other people.

Anger Management Relaxation Techniques

Anger can be managed using a variety of techniques, but most of them will not work if they are used casually. One must commit to using and practicing them to have chances of a positive effect.

Controlled deep breathing

The breathing rate and heartbeat rate of an individual increase when one becomes emotionally aroused. One can reverse these effects by slowing down the breathing rate deliberately and relaxing the tensed muscles systematically. One is able to maintain control using these relaxing practices.

When one is upset, he/she finds him/herself taking quick, shallow breaths. Continuation of this shallow breathing only exacerbates anger. Instead, one should take action to control the breathing and deliberately relax the tensed muscles in order to calm down. In order to get the full benefits of this technique, one should set aside at least 15 minutes to do this exercise. Selecting less time will make the practice ineffective.

Practicing slow breathing

First, initiate the relaxation efforts by taking several deep yet slow breaths in a row. Ensure that every time, you breathe out for twice as long as you breathed in. This is to mean, count slowly to three when breathing in and then count to 6 while breathing out slowly. Longer breaths translate to better results.

During the breathing technique, take time to observe the movement of air within the lungs. Again, open the lungs and chest cavity, and breathe in fully and deeply. This breath should first fill the belly, then the chest and later, the upper chest, right below the shoulders. Feel the ribs and lungs expand with air. Next, take time to feel how the ribs return to the original place as you exhale. Practice this technique for as long as you can.

This slow and deliberate breathing will help one to return their breathing to regular rates whenever they are angry. Controlled breathing patterns help one to control many aspects of the body. Keeping in mind that all the things in the body are connected, slow, and deep breathing will help you to control the heartbeat rate, the tension in some muscles, and in some cases, aches.

In a number of events, anger manifests itself as muscle tension. Usually, this tension collects itself along the neck and shoulders and might last long after the anger is gone. If the neck is tense, it is essential to practice the muscle relaxation technique which involves slowly and gently rolling the neck side to side. Roll the head from one shoulder to the other with coordinated breaths; roll to the side while exhaling and to the center while inhaling. Repeat the technique until the tension in the muscles starts to fade. The tension in the shoulders can be released by careful and deliberate shrugging and releasing several times.

Another practice that may help with shoulder muscles relaxation is rolling them backward and forwards. Using the breathing and muscle relation technique will help one to relax. Use the anger diary to check for areas that feel tensed during moments of anger and use the relaxation techniques to sort them out.

Progressive muscle relaxation

For some people, the relaxation techniques might not work—therefore, they may try the opposite, which involves:

- Tightening and tensing the stressed muscles for about 15 seconds and then releasing them slowly. If you feel any pain due to these techniques, ensure that you release the muscles immediately.

- Move from one group of muscles to the next until all the tensed ones have received the cycle of tense and release. With a little practice, one can use the tension and release technique on the whole body in a few minutes. Tensing and relaxing technique has been found to be more effective than the relaxation technique only.

- Whichever technique one is using, he/she should give about 20 to 30 minutes before the achievement of an entirely calm state. During this time, one needs to keep breathing very deep and regular. He/she should also tell self that it will be better soon in order to keep going.

Relaxation techniques such as the ones described above ensure that a person does not focus too much on being angry. These techniques give one time to think about the circumstances surrounding their upset moment and also time to generate fresh solutions to the problems he/she is facing.

Reality Testing as an Anger Management Tool

Anger is an emotion that makes people unable to think clearly during upset moments. When one is angry, he/she tends to make decisions about a situation or case right away. These people tend to spend more time brooding over how they feel and how the situation has affected their normal life rather than looking at things critically. One will have a better chance of keeping self under control if he/she can avoid looking only at the inward side but also assess the situation from the perspectives of other people. Do not look too much at how the people or thing made you feel; instead, focus on understanding all the details.

Even though it can be hard, one should squeeze the message out of the situation even when the anger impulse is making the best of the situation. It is important to consider the message that the anger is passing to you and what you can learn from it. Which aspect of the particular situation is making you angry? Why? What can you do to improve the circumstances? Then use the relaxation techniques to reduce the heat of the moment.

Remember that you do not have to respond to the situation right away especially if anger is taking over. Most of the situations are flexible enough for one to take some time, gather the right facts and thoughts, and then respond. Take time to think about the situation before acting. You may also take time talk things over with a trusted person before making a decision. The more one approaches a troubling situation in a relaxed and prepared manner, the higher the chances of getting positive results. A calm mind will help one get what they want.

Reality Testing

In most countries, an accused criminal is assumed to be innocent until there is enough proof of guilt. However, angry people do not make this assumption; rather, they assume that the people who upset them are actually guilty. Angry people tend to blame others and sometimes themselves for the things that go wrong. The angry persons tend to make the assumption that the target being blamed has actually caused things to go wrong. However, this is not always the case because the accused person can be an innocent bystander who got caught up in the situation. In order to manage the anger better, it is better to slow down and make serious considerations rather than acting on the first impulse. Reality tests will help you to know if the anger is justified and if the person receiving the wrath is actually guilty. The first step for building viable reality testing habits involve giving up the assumption that the first impression of the situation is always accurate. It is hard to know the truth at first glance especially when one is angry. In most cases, we see only one side of the story (our own). The reality is usually more complicated than what we see and appreciate.

For the sake of illustration, imagine that people believe that earth is the center of the universe and that the sun and the moon actually revolved around it. People in the ancient world also believed that the world is flat and if you walked far enough, you would get to the edge and fall over. Even now, without the right knowledge, one would merely perceive the world as a flat surface. The pure sense of life can deceive us; therefore, we should rely on techniques and analysis to figure out the truth of the matter.

The first people to suggest that the world was round and the earth was not the center were seen as madmen. However, after years of study and analysis, we all agree that the world is round and the earth is not the center. All people needed to realize is the truth was proof. Angry people should realize that their first conclusion might be as wrong as every other misguided thought and evidence is needed before they can place judgments. Conclusively, angry people need to pause and gather complete information before they can pass judgment in order to make better conclusions.

Black-and-white thinking

Once you understand that the world is a complicated place, it becomes easier to accept that the first expression is not always right. In the moment of anger, one might not be able to capture the accurate and complete picture of a troubling situation. Recognizing complexity can be challenging for some angry people who are in the habit of identifying the world as a black and white place. Majority of angry people talk about the world in polarized generalities whereby they insist that things must always be done in certain ways, or that people should never do certain things. They also tend to concentrate on the negative side rather than seeking the good in things and acknowledging positivity. These people tend to jump into conclusions at a rapid pace and will rarely bother to verify whether or not their understanding is correct. These mentalities of black and white need to be spoken down in order to recognize the shades of gray before anger management progress occurs in a lasting way.

Talking it out helps

When one is open to the possibilities that the first impression is not always right, there are a number of ways to test the impressions in order to gain a better and more complete understanding. The best way to test the reality involves talking to other people who have experience with such circumstances. What did they think happened before they figure out the truth? How did they find out the facts? What was the actual cause of the problem? When you consult other people and, they see the situation as you do, that is, you have been harmed, then you are more justified to feel angry. If the other people see the situation differently, then you are not justified to accuse the other person. The input of other people can help you to appreciate the complex nature of a situation.

Count to ten

The next alternative of reality test method besides consulting g others is to use the rule of counting to ten before you act. This venerable rule is also known as giving the other person the benefit of the doubt. As the anger rises because of the situation, one should put breaks and count slowly. This may be combined with breathing and relaxation techniques. One should do what he/she can to calm down. Next, he/she should take the time to look for alternative explanations that might help to understand the situation more comprehensively.

For instance, if a person is driving in front of you really slowly and it is a free highway, you may first think that they are doing it to stall you and block you from getting to your destination in time. The first impulse will be to scream at the driver for being slow and incompetent. By counting to ten before you can let out your thoughts, you give yourself time to check the alternatives of the causes of slow driving. For instance, the car might be having mechanical problems, or the driver might be exhausted. Maybe the driver has been given a number of speeding tickets recently, therefore, slowly driving so as to avoid another one. If one of these options turn out to be true, then it will be hard to stay mad at the driver even though you are still stuck behind him/her.

Chapter 8: Anger Management and Communication

There are different types of communication styles applied by people. Angry people usually take certain postures and communication stances when they communicate with other people. In psychology, there are terms used to describe these communication stances, each taking on its own motto:

1. **Aggressive communication** - In this posture, the person says, "I am worthy buy you are not."
2. **Passive communication** - The person using this posture normally says, "I don't count."
3. **Passive-aggressive communication** - In this posture, a person says "I am worthy. You are not worthy, but I will not tell you."
4. **Assertive communication** - The people in this posture say, "I am worthy, and so are you."

It is evident that most angry people use more passive aggressive and aggressive postures. The people that use aggressive posture have higher chances of starting an argument—thus failing to reach the goal they intended to pursue. Being passive in communication is also bad in communication because it gives off the aura of weakness therefor inviting further aggression. Assertive communication is more useful and balanced since it takes into account the feelings of all the parties in the picture. It is the only posture that communicates respect for everyone. Assertive communication is most probably the best way of ensuring that every person has their needs accounted for. It is therefore very imperative that one learns how to communicate assertively rather than aggressively or passive-aggressively in order to pass and constructively receive messages.

People who have a habit of being aggressive tend to misinterpret the meaning of being assertive. To be specific, these people tend to confuse aggression and assertiveness. They think that their actions and words are assertive. The two communication styles can involve persuasion and fierce communication. However, there are fundamental things that differ for instance; the aggressive communicators tend to take the defensive while the assertive people stand up for their rights and themselves without crossing the lines of others. Typically, aggressive communication will berate and attack others regardless of the situation. On the other hand, assertive communication will only use anger and fierceness when defending. Assertive communication does not cross the lines of others unnecessarily.

Anger Management and Request Making

The style of communication that one uses determines the ability of a person to make requests. Normally, people who use aggressive communication technique have challenges making requests in an effective manner. Remember that angry people normally use aggressive communication and thus will fail at making requests. Because they already feel entitled, the angry people make a wrongful assumption that every person should do their bidding. They, therefore, will not make requests under the assumption that the people around them know when to make requests and how to make them. Even when they try to make requests, they make them in a way that it sounds like a demand, which then provokes anger in others and will not happily carry out the request. An effective request should involve clarity, emotional transparency and respectfulness.

Clarity refers to the making of a well-formed request which states clearly the wants and needs of the individual. When a request lacks clarity, it becomes hard to fulfill and will most probably lead to anger, frustration, and stress. This is more so the case when requests are put forward and interpreted as commands. A clear request needs to be stated explicitly and must give clear answers to certain questions that is; who, what and when.

Emotional transparency involves stating the real feelings instead of making accusations. For instance, if one tells the other, "You, idiot—you are so insensitive. What is it with you that you must always forget? Where is the milk I told you to buy? Can't you even remember such small things?" can you feel the intensity of the defense in the statement? The person is avoiding stating the real feelings and accusing the other of being an idiot. Such a request will turn a sympathetic crowd off very fast. The request lacks emotional transparency, therefore failing to appeal to the other person. Emotional transparency involves the willingness to share real feelings. The speaker sounds rude and self-centered. But if we pay closer attention to the feelings, we will sense that the speaker feels left out or neglected.

It will be better if one states his/her requests with emotional transparency, sharing the real reason for the request. That transparency is likely to motivate the listener into acting. In the example given above, we can rephrase "I feel like to do not care about me when you forget to pick something for me. Please remember to keep it for me next time." In this phrase, the speaker makes it clear that his/her feelings are hurt when the other person forgets to deliver as requested. This result in two good things, first, the message is clear, and secondly, it leaves no room for the listener to take a defensive stand. When requests are made with emotional transparency, clarity, and respect, there are high chances that the listener will take it to heart.

Respectfulness involves forming the request in a manner that makes the person want to comply. Respect makes people feel honored therefore are more likely to assist the person in making the request. When making requests, statements such as: "If it is not too much to ask, could you please…" or "Would you please help me…" or "I would really appreciate if you…"

There is a good request formula that helps one to pass information clearly called the *Assertive Request Formula*. This formula involves three parts that add up to one complete statement:

"I feel _____ when you _____ because _____."

It is, however, very important that one makes sure he/she does not accuse the other when making the request. For instance, one should not say "I feel that you are silly." The 'I feel section' is about how you feel. The formula does not work on accusations. This is because you will have made an accusation and made the other person to take a defensive stance based on the aggressive attacking statement. Talk about yourself in order to get better results. For instance, you can say "I feel deserted when you fail to call me and let me know that you will be late because I get worried that you might be in danger."

Chapter 9: Selecting an Anger Management Program

In the scientific study of emotions, anger has received less attention compared to other problems such as depression and anxiety. However, there are a number of anger management programs that have been identified to help reduce and manage anger effectively. Most have them have successfully reduced unhealthy anger and help the users to improve adaptive coping skills. Unfortunately, not all programs have been proven to work—therefore, one needs to make some consideration before settling for any of them. The quality of the program varies a lot, and while some are grounded on solid scientific research, others are just guesswork and potentially harmful.

According to scientists, the best anger management programs are based on cognitive behavioral frameworks. Summarily, the cognitive behavioral theories, state that the human emotional reactions are mostly influenced by our interpretation of events more than the events themselves. For instance, if one gets angry because of the driving speed of the person in front of them, it is not because of the driving style, rather, it is the belief and interpretation that the other person could do better. The anger management programs that are based on cognitive behavioral theories tend to pay attention to teaching individuals how to control and reduce their physiological and emotional arousal, thinking in less provocative ways. They teach the individual how to think and express anger in productive ways. These programs will put emphasis on the development of self-control strategies.

When selecting a program, here are some of the things that one may consider:

i. Programs based on cognitive behavioral theories tend to have reliable research support and are more cost-effective and brief. Many of these programs can be completed in 2 to 3 months.

ii. There are some practices that have been disapproved, but some people still use them. For instance, those programs that allow for aggressive and uncontrolled expression of anger such as striking things with bats and punching pillows and bags are discouraged. They might provide relief for the short term, but in the end, there is a high chance of applying aggressive anger in the future.

iii. Select a treatment provider that you are comfortable with. Just because a person is using an approved program does not mean that they know how to apply it. It is therefore important that you find a good provider.

Depending on personal needs, one may choose to work with a professional counselor or a counseling support group to learn how to control anger. One may also choose to work on his/her own using a self-study resource of choice. One should be warned however that changing a long term habit can be hard; therefore, a lot of commitment is required. A good support system will help you to make and maintain real change in behavior. As such, if you are truly serious about making a change in the way you handle anger, it is better to participate in a support group. It will help you keep track of the changes you make. A self-study program is good, but you will be better off in a group that has your interests at heart. Formal programs help one to stick to a structured guideline for change, give one motivation to continue working towards his/her goals even when the desire to quit is overwhelming.

Below is a list of different types of anger management programs that one may choose from:

Individual and Group Therapy

In this style of anger management, one works with a psychologist or a licensed professional either individually or in a group setting. The best thing about working with a therapist is that you get someone to observe and analyze your behavior and progress. The therapist gets to check your progress from an unbiased perspective and thus will help with your tests for reality. In group therapy, the other members will help you keep track of your progress. You will also have people to compare notes. An anger management therapist will also offer you more than one ways of checking your anger. In the event that one program fails, he/she will suggest other ways that might work.

Remember that not every therapist knows how to use the programs as designed and you might get worse in the long term. As such, it is advisable that you select a therapist that is right for you. A cognitive behavioral therapist is best for anger management because he/she is better informed about emotion control. There are other qualities that you will need to look at before you settle for any therapist. Ideally, a licensed therapist will have the right training to help you apply the anger management therapies and techniques. Others will have special practice for management of anger.

Typically, an anger management course will not unfold like a traditional therapy session; rather it will be like a class. In these therapy sessions, the participants will be helped to become more conscious of their cognitive, emotional and physical responses to conflicts and anger. Depending on personal needs, the therapist will choose whether to work with you on meditation and breathing exercises to reduce the arousal of anger. He/she may also choose to help you apply a safe and appropriate physical and emotional technique to release anger. The training may also include communication skills and cognitive restructuring.

The effect of therapy can take different time for different people. On average, progress will be seen after 8 to 10 sessions. The progress is partly determined by your personal effort and dedication which involves; the regular attendance of therapy sessions, how deeply you take the lessons, and the seriousness you put in practicing your homework.

Anger Management Classes

The anger management classes are usually available through employers, a variety of organizations, and different sections of the community. Anger management classes differ in quality and length. While some of the classes spread across a long period of time, there are others that last only for a short while such as one weekend. Whatever you do, it is better to pick a program that lasts for longer than one weekend; it will give you more sustainable information. The longer the class, the more the information you will gather for your changing process. However, regardless of the length of the program, you will be assigned homework projects and test quizzes to track the progress through your course.

It is important that you keep track of your personal needs and think carefully about your changing needs. If your anger arises more with work colleagues at workplaces, maybe an anger management seminar would benefit. If your anger is against a spouse, then you would benefit more from a couple's therapy. Whichever path you choose, make sure that the selected path is approved and will guide you towards your goals.

Self-Study

You can learn ways to manage anger on your own in a variety of ways. There are video and audio recordings that allow one to complete anger management programs in his/her own space and time and at a personal speed. Some of these groups offer the person an online platform to contribute to, support through email or phone, and even support chat groups.

If you want a more specialized approach of managing your anger, for instance, a program designed for a working mother, or for a corporate executive, there is a large collection of resources in the libraries and online. You may do some more research before settling for a program or class.

Following Through the Anger Management Program

A day will come when you will stop planning to manage anger and actually follow it through. Regardless of whether you pursue your anger management goals personally or through a support group, one day, you will be needed actually to change your behavior. Because it requires a lot of work to change a behavior that has developed over time, it is important that you actually commit to your course and stick to it until you see positive results. There are a number of strategies that you may follow to get to good anger management. These strategies give structure to the program that you chose, and they will help you to sustain commitment. If you do not follow a program systematically, you will not benefit from an anger management program, even if it is the best and most reliable technique.

Stick to a program for as long as recommended. You will have higher chances of seeing changes if you follow a professionally designed anger management program; get a good lead into the program. Although a personally designed program may work, it is better to spend your time focusing on how to change your behavior rather than how to design a management technique. In most cases, a professionally designed program will offer you support on a personal and group level. A group leader will help you sustain progress even when the temptation to quit is running high. The support you receive can either be emotional or technical. As you get motivated, you will also motivate others. In the process, you will sometime give other people the help they need. This motivates you to pursue your own.

Some people know well that a group program will not work for them and others may fail to locate a well-suited class, therefore, will opt to make their own plan. It is still advisable for them to follow a laid out schedule when making a personalized one. It is also important that you select a person or two to help you check your progress. In the simplest terms, having a structured plan will help you succeed in managing your anger.

Cognitive Behavioral Therapy for Anger Management

One of the most used types of psychotherapy is cognitive behavioral therapy. This therapy is purposed for treatment in that it helps the angry person to recognize the negative and self-defeating thoughts that are firing the emotion. This form of therapy has actually proven to the most effective for anger management. Normally, ineffective ways of managing anger impulses can lead to patterns of bottling up feelings until they explode leading to serious problems both at work and other relations. Again, poor stress management can increase resentment and anger, and in the end, one will not know how to express such emotions effectively.

Cognitive behavioral therapy for anger management may include:
- Mindfulness training
- Distress tolerance training,
- Cognitive restructuring of dysfunctional thoughts

- Assertiveness skill building
- Emotion regulation training

In simple terms, CBT will help you to understand how to change your thought, behaviors, and feelings. By targeting the way that you react to the situations, this therapy helps you to act more effectively. In fact, it teaches one to feel better about a situation even when he/she is unable to change it. There are a number of benefits that make CBT worthwhile including the fact that it is goal oriented. CBT is focused on the present situations; it is brief, well research and involves team activities.

Cognitive Behavioral Therapy – Goal-Oriented

Unlike a good number of talk therapies, CBT is a problem-solving therapy that helps one to achieve his/her goals. Goals can be anything from getting along with a boss to being in a lasting relationship. One could seek anger management help with the intention of reducing feelings of depression or anxiety. Once the patient has achieved his/her goals, he/she will work together with the therapist and decide if there is anything else they are required to do.

Cognitive Behavioral Therapy – Focused on the Present

CBT typically concentrates on the current situations and present difficulties that are distressing. The here and now angle help the patient to solve current problems more effectively and quickly. Identifying the individual challenges and focusing on them one by one in a structured and consistent manner results in the achievement of greater treatment gains, and reaching them in a shorter timeframe than other talk therapies.

Cognitive Behavioral Therapy – Active

Cognitive behavioral therapy requires collaboration and teamwork. The patient and the therapist have to work together to solve problems. Instead of waiting for the problem to go away after listening to an endless talk, the patient has the opportunity to make suggestions in the sessions. There are self-help assignments and tools that one uses between the sessions. They help the patient to speed up the healing process. Each session looks a different way of thinking differently. The patient unlearns unwanted reactions while identifying new ways of managing anger.

Cognitive Behavioral Therapy – Brief

CBT is limited by time, meaning that once you and the therapist have identified that you have improved, you can end the session or put it on hold for the period you want. Consequently, CBT is shorter than the other traditional talk therapies which can last years. A good number of people finish CBT in a few months. It is important to note that not all people respond quickly to therapy. Some people will need additional therapy to create a lasting change. The patients with serious chronicle challenges may need a long timeframe, anywhere between 6 months and several years. However, even for the patients that need more time in therapy, CBT is still preferred.

Cognitive Behavioral Therapy – Well-Researched

This therapy is one of the few that have been proven scientifically. Researchers have found that it is effective. Making big changes can be very challenging; therefore, one will need a lot of support. A well-researched therapy will help you to manage anger more effectively.

The steps followed in cognitive behavioral therapy include:
1. Awareness of your emotions and thoughts surrounding anger trigger
2. Identification of the circumstances or situations in your life that lead to anger
3. Acknowledgment of negative and inaccurate thought patterns
4. Learning healthier and positive thought patterns

There are very few risks associated with cognitive behavioral therapy, and there are plenty of benefits. One should be warned that he/she might be required to walk through his/her past and painful memories but will do so under good guidance.

Other Treatment Program Options

There are several options available for people who seek to manage anger including inpatient and outpatient treatment. Modern treatment options are targeted and effective, and in most cases, they will give results in as few as 6 to 8 weeks. As one goes through these options, he/she should know that anger is not something that can be gotten rid of. It is a healthy part of life shared by all people everywhere. The aim of these program options is to help one manage anger before it becomes destructive or results in all sorts of personal problems. You cannot cure anger, but you can manage the effect and intensity. Some therapeutic strategies can help one to reduce reactivity. One can even learn to apply more patience in the face of situations and people he/she cannot control.

Most of the therapies concentrate on problem-solving skills, communication skills, and avoidance of certain situations, humor, and cognitive behavior. It is possible for one to work through anger without help from outside, but a therapist will help to move through the program faster.

Residential / Inpatient Anger Management Treatment Programs

If anger is affecting the day to day life of a person, then an inpatient or residential anger management center may be recommended. It could be important for one to stay with a team of dedicated treatment staff under controlled conditions if he/she:
- Is in trouble with the law because of anger issues
- Lashing out at a spouse or children especially physically
- Is experiencing constant and uncontrolled arguments with coworkers and family members
- Is threatening violence to people and property
- Believes that everything will be fine if he/she suppressed anger
- Loses control of self when angry

Since the aim of anger management treatment is to gather the tools necessary to express the emotion in a constructive, safe, and healthy way, a therapist or professional is best suited to help.

Benefits of In-House Anger Management Treatments

Residential anger management treatment helps one to learn how to gain control over frustration and anger. An in-house therapist can help a patient to recognize dangerous situations become more aware of the warning signs when rage is impending. Additionally, residential treatment will help you to understand ways of avoiding anger suppression which will lead to depression, hypertension, anxiety and heart troubles. Most importantly, residential treatment helps one to develop management strategies away from the outside world and triggers.

There are different aspects that one must consider before selecting a residential facility. Just because it is a treatment facility does not mean that it has to have sterile and inhumane conditions. A number of these luxury facilities are comfortable and serene. A good environment will facilitate a positive mental mood thus help one to learn faster.

Executive Anger Management Program

These programs are designed for executives, lawyers, physicians, and other professionals who want discretion and privacy and wish to benefit from a one on one program. Effective anger management strategies will not only benefit an individual executive when interacting with employees, customers, or patients; it will also help them to make sound organizational policies. When a professional is able to deal with anger and stress positively, he/she is better positioned to instruct and work with others.

In executive anger management programs, the individuals can expect to learn ways to:
1. Communicate directly and respectfully;
2. Restore trust;
3. Repair broken relationships find positive resolutions for stressed and stressful people and situations;
4. Control emotional reactiveness;
5. Resolve conflicts in a healthy way; and
6. Empathize with customers and coworkers.

Outpatient Anger Treatment Programs

In some cases, a person is willing to go for an anger management program but not in a position to attend an inpatient session. For instance, if a job is too demanding, or there is a young family involved, one might not manage a residential program. Again, if your anger issue does not pose physical threats to people or things, then you might not need a residential program. An outpatient program is best suited for such a person. Many outpatient programs offer intense counseling for individuals, and they typically last for six to eight weeks. They also help the patient to prepare for more follow up care at home. With outpatient programs, one has to deal with external situations and people because the environment is not controlled. One will thus benefit from supportive friends and family.

Finding the Best Anger Management Treatment Facility

Once you are ready to take control of your anger and have decided to seek help, it is important to consider a number of things. If you opt for a facility, look for one that offers comprehensive assessment, appropriate treatment and follow up services. Speak to the professionals in the facility directly and ask them about their qualifications and experiences. It might sound like a lot, but you will be better off knowing the methods and expected results rather than doing guesswork. Express all your concerns to them and ensure that the facilitators explain the full costs of the program. Some health insurance covers help one to pay part of such expenses.

You will gain more from the program you choose if:
1. You treat your therapist as a partner rather than a supervisor;
2. You are open about your thoughts and feelings;
3. You stay consistent and follow the treatment plan;
4. You remember that determination and patience lead to results;
5. You communicate well with your team, especially when facing challenges; and
6. You do your homework.

The Contractual Commitment

It is advisable for one to draw up a contract that lays out the specific plan detailing out the things, you want to practice in the course of the anger management program. The best part of signing such a contract is that you will have made for yourself support and structure to follow. These two aspects are important for your success. Print out the contract on a page and sign with ink. If you have people supporting you on your quest, you may ask them to sign as witnesses to your progress. You may also consider posting the signed contract in a public place for instance in your house so that the people around you can understand what you are after and even help you. Going public will strengthen your commitment and help the people around you to support you.

The details you need to include in the contract have to be very specific. For instance, you need to write down:
    a. Your goals - what you hope to gain from the program
    b. The plan - what you need to do in order to reach your goals
    c. When and how you will practice the things you have laid out

When making the contract, be very specific with the goals, avoid using generalities such as 'I want to stop overreacting.' Such open-ended goals are impossible to measure in a specific way and thus leave too much room to jump from one end to the other with a false feeling of accomplishment. Instead of setting some unrealistic and unspecific goals, describe real situations which make you angry and make you lay out how you intend to change them. Write down the techniques that you will use to confront those situations. Repeat the techniques if you must. Repeating things helps one to remember and understand.

Take some time out

In the contract, ensure that you include taking time out. This means that you willingly step away from a situation that is forcing anger out of you. For instance, if you disagree with your spouse, make an agreement that you will walk away from the tight spot and make space to cool down. Keep in mind the fact that if you do not walk away, the chances are that the situation will get out of hand. Take some time to step away, think critically, and calm down.

Breaks can help you sort the situation while in a better frame of mind. Similarly, if family demands are habitually overwhelming you when you get home after work, make a point of taking a break before you get to the house. During this time, ensure that you relax. Do not mistake drinking alcohol as a way of relaxing; it is an unhealthy way of decompressing. One good way could be to go to the gym or to take a yoga class. Just give yourself a buffer zone- a space to do something you are interested in. Taking a break will help you relax such that once you get home; you will be able to appreciate the good things in your family without being hostile or cranky. A few minutes of some me time will help you to handle situations when you get home.

In the contract, agree that you will practice relaxation and breathing techniques on a regular basis. It is preferable for you to practice them daily. Learning how to stay calm requires you to understand Ways through which you react less violently regardless of the stress involved in the situation. Consequently, you will be required to learn how to relax skillfully. Some of the most effective relaxation techniques that you can use to calm yourself down include meditation, deep breathing as well as physical exercises. With practice and patience, these techniques become a proactive way of minimizing your general anger arousal.

Examining thought

In your contract, include a section for reviewing thoughts. As seen earlier, the first thoughts that occur to one when angry are normally judgmental and imperfect because they are based on incomplete information. When you simply focus on the incomplete impressions, chances are, you will attack the people around you, and this will not be a smart move. Rather than just going off when mad, promise yourself that you will critically and carefully assess the situations that provoke anger. The best time for you to assess your anger is during the time out session, just before the anger subsides or gets out of control. Learn to see the situation types that trigger your anger and the thoughts that occur to you when furious. Make serious considerations as to whether it is good for you to react when angry. Refrain from acting out of the automatic emotional reactions (which are normally wrong) and think critically and logically about the situations.

Assertive communication

In the contract, clearly state, that you will take some time every day to practice assertive speaking skills. You could look for a book about assertive communication and read it. Write down the things that you normally say to people in an aggressive way. Then rewrite them in an assertive way. Practice the assertive sentences with people, in front of a mirror or during role-play sessions. If you sense that you will be getting into a situation that will anger you, practice the assertive statements in advance; it will help you to deal with the real circumstance.

Besides practicing assertive communication which mostly involves passing your message, it is also important that you practice listening to other people. There is a need to become a skillful listener who participates in the conversation constructively. In the end, you will expand your chances of getting what you want from other people.

Contract duration

It is important to have a timeframe for hour anger management program. Ideally, it should not be too long; neither should it be too short. It could run through the timeframe of the program you select. However, a better option is to break the contract down to shorter but linked periods. For instance, a contract could last for one to five days – or the duration that suits your plan best. Some people start with a contract lasting for twenty-four hours while others choose a few days. When one contract ends, then the person writes a new one, making new commitments.

The advantage of short contracts is that they allow you to adapt them to the changes you are experiencing. As you learn new techniques, the renewed contract allows you to evaluate your practices. Short contracts will also allow you to feel successful when you have accomplished the short term goal—thus giving you the motivation to pursue the next one. Reward yourself for every achieved contract, have time to feel good about it, and then get into the next one. Whether you settle for a day by day contract or a longer period one, you should sign it and ensure that the witnesses also confirm your achievements. Store the contract, or post it in a public place as a reminder.

Let people help you

Your family, partners, friends, and even associates will be in a better position to recognize the moment you are getting angry. As such, it is advisable to include them in the plan if possible. You can agree with your assistance team on a signal they can give you when they see you starting to slip into the old habit of aggressive expression. Once you spot the signal, ensure that you change your behavior; otherwise, the anger will escalate. Some techniques that could help you avoid this escalation include taking some time out or agreeing to handle the situation later when you are emotionally stable.

Reward yourself

Rewards act as good motivation sources. It is therefore important that you include your rewards in the contract. Have a reward for every time you achieve a set goal in the contract. However, the reward should be healthy and sensible, preferably, something that you can do without in the event that you do not achieve your goals. It should also be a gift that makes you look forward to winning, one that you will feel good if you get. For instance, you could treat yourself to something you have been looking forward to such as attending an opera show.

Chapter 10: The Use of Anger Management Techniques: Putting Them Together

We have looked at an array of information and a variety of techniques that one can use to manage and develop healthy anger in the topics above. One may want to practice these techniques in isolation, but it does not necessarily have to be. You may combine any number of techniques that work for you so long as they help to achieve goals.

When you are provoked to anger by a particular situation, stop and make considerations. Reflect before responding. The following steps summarize the anger management techniques:

1. Immediately you feel angry, stop your line of thought and action. Once you recognize that your anger is rising, change or hold your thoughts and actions, you could think about something else that is more pleasurable. If imagery works for you, try to picture a red stop sign.

2. When anger starts to rise, the mechanisms of the body begin to change too. For instance, the heartbeat rate increases, and the blood pressure rises. To counter these physical signs, use the relaxation and breathing technique. You can choose a word to recite in order to invoke the state of calmness. For instance, you could use the words calm and cool repeatedly.

3. Give the situation a thought and try to identify the triggers that set your anger off. Ask yourself questions such as; what thoughts are occupying my head right now? What am I feeling? How is my body responding? I'm I considering the whole scenario or just the first impression? What do I want? Do I want revenge and is it really worth it? What if I act aggressively? What consequences do I stand to face? In what other ways can I respond to the situation rather than acting out of anger? Will they make the situation worse or better?

4. Once you have made the above considerations, consider the way you want to respond. It is better if you work to identify an assertive response more than an aggressive one.

5. Respond. After making all the considerations, thinking, rethinking, and checking the facts, talking to someone about the situation etc., when you have the details right, respond.

In most cases, the heat of the moment when one is angry makes the situation look as if it needs a very urgent answer. You will realize that the situation does not really need an immediate drastic response; it is better if you take some time and reconsider. The urgency of the situation is usually an illusion, and once you calm down, it becomes clearer. The intense arousal of the moment contributes to the impatience.

When you feel the anger rising, and the heat of the moment getting too intense, it would help a lot to ask for some time out and use some of the anger management techniques to analyze the situation. While disengaging from the anger situation, use a polite statement to excuse yourself such as "I feel upset now, let me step away for a while and continue with this conversation later." The time out will interrupt your anger process, and once you get back to the situation, your mind will be refreshed and more accommodative. It is better if you re-approach the case in an assertive rather than aggressive way.

If the situation does not allow you to take a break, try the following steps:

1. Avoid accusations. Instead of telling the other person about their faults in an aggressive way, use the 'I' statement to explain your feelings and make a request. The goal of communication is to let other people know your stand, not belittling them to beating them up.

2. While talking, do not stare at the person straight in the eye, rather, make intermittent eye contact at intervals. Too much staring during a confrontation comes off as aggression while interval eye contact shows courage and the will to stand up for what you believe.

3. When listening to other people, ensure that you practice active listening. Avoid the "yes, but" statement. This normally diverts the attention of the other person to you. Consequently, if the 'yes but' continues, the other person feels left out.

4. When talking, assess if your needs have been heard. Do you think that the person you were passing the message to understand all you said? In a heated

moment, the person you are communicating with might misunderstand the message because he/she focuses too much on the arousal. In case you realize that he/she did not understand your message, then restate it in a different way. Keep in mind that the person might actually be too angry to understand you; therefore, you might be required to slow down and allow then to rant. Not every angry person is able to use the control techniques that you have learned. If communication turns out to be impossible, it is important that you disengage and continue another time.

5. Whatever you do, avoid getting into a premature reaction. It will take time and practice to solve things with patience, but in the end, it will be worth the while. Buy more time when angry, stall your answer, wait a little longer. If your choice is to lose your temper or leave, choose to leave. It is better to retain control than win through aggression.

Practice Makes It Perfect

Remember that it is very hard and probably impossible to learn how to manage anger overnight. However, there will be many opportunities in your life whereby you can practice different techniques. You may also learn to apply them more if you exercise through role-playing. These practices will help to simulate and control your triggers.

Role-playing can be done on a personal basis or with a partner. However, role play applies best if you have a support group; one where you share the goals. Use the list of triggers to come up with situations that present the anger management challenges. If you are not working with a partner, stand in front of a mirror and speak to yourself. It might sound crazy, but professional actors do it most of the time to enhance their acting skills. Take a role as if you are talking to someone you are angry with. Get into the character as realistically as you can. Make your imagination as vivid as possible. Speak out loud and imagine the most realistic replies. Initially, it will feel awkward talking to yourself loudly in front of a mirror but with time, the anxiety will go, and you will feel more comfortable with the practice.

If you have access to partners and groups to play the roles with, the better, it will be easier to keep track of your development when other people are involved. It is easier to direct the emotions at someone, even though it is just an act. Stay in control for as long as you can and maintain character. Practice makes perfect.

Anger and Advocacy

What makes you angry? Is it a wrong treatment in the office? Or a particular disease that affects someone you love? The fact that drought is killing people? Are there any reports of child labor?

Good anger has helped people find solutions for many challenges across the centuries. For instance, anger made people fight slavery. This emotion made freedom fighters to face their oppressors. Anger also made women fight for their rights to vote and work. High hospital bills made people fight for insurance.

How can you use your anger in a good way? Turn it into advocacy. Start a movement that fights for or against a particular course. If your anger stems from the images of children in certain locations in the world dying of anger, start a course that sensitizes people of such. If it is because of a disease that took a loved one away from you because you did not have enough information, start a platform where people can learn more about it.

Focusing too much on your anger will only cause resentment. Look for ways to bless others with your energy. Advocacy might appear hard at first, but in due time, you will have course worth your energy.

Chapter 11: Relapses and Anger Treatment

While one is working towards overcoming an anger problem, there are times when relapses will occur. The person will probably get into earlier anger habits such as becoming inappropriately angry, belligerent, and aggressive. Backslides, slips, and lapses are virtually almost inevitable in the anger management programs—therefore, one will have to plan for them. The most important thing is refusing to give up.

No matter how challenging it is, do not allow a lapse to be your excuse of quitting an anger program. Treat failures as learning experiences. Examine the events that triggered the relapse carefully and learn how the situation occurred. Which part of your anger management plan was insufficient for the situation? The information you gather from this analysis will help you to fix your program so that it works better next time.

In the process of planning for relapses, it is important that you look for problematic events in advance and mentally prepare for them. If you have not yet gone for professional help, it would be time to seek it. If you have gone through counseling and treatment programs, booster sessions can work wonders to help you go about your business. Booster sessions involve going back to your therapist and getting extra assistance on your issue. This booster session might include reviewing the anger management strategies you are using, checking the current stressors and getting an objective opinion on your next step. Booster sessions do not indicate that you have failed.

Mentality About Relapses

There is a high probability that most people will slip up or make a relapse. One thing to look out for is your thoughts towards the slip-up. Mentalities make things better or worse for us. If you beat yourself up because of a relapse, you will most probably have more problems with anger. People often think that abusive self-criticism is a source of motivation, but it actually is not. There are some rational and irrational thoughts identified in people who have lapses, and it has been observed that a line of thought can determine if the person will recover or keep relapsing. Some of these thoughts include:

Irrational	Rational
I will get nowhere with this.	I have improved greatly in many ways. I have learned many new skills and can actually manage my anger better
I am a horrible creature.	I am human and prone to errors.
I'll never improve.	My trend has been good. This is just a setback that I'll overcome.

Stick to your plan.

Anger management involves different techniques and skills such as deep breathing and relaxation, assertive communication, identifying the triggers ad countering them, forgiveness, change of mentality and disengaging from brooding. With time, you will be tempted to drop some of the techniques that feel like they have completed their role. That might actually be the beginning of your relapse. Do not stop using a coping skill just because you feel like it's out of service. Keep practicing it. If you had dropped one skill, pick it again. It will take a very long time for you to stop using these techniques and even then, you might be required to pull them out of the store and practice them at one point or the other.

Another step to recovering from relapses is to check for those strategies and techniques that you failed to pay attention to. Those assignments that you did not complete assessing are where the weakness might be lying there. You have nothing to lose by checking your former work.

Seek feedback.

The people that surround you such as spouses, family, trusted friends could help you to track the cause of your relapse. Simply, they can be your lifeguards in the anger management quest. When you experience a relapse, you may ask them to help you point out the point at which you relapsed and the causes. These people can help you spot a regression before it gets out of hand.

However, it is important that you understand these people will only help you if you ask. Ask them to look for things that indicate you are getting out of sorts. They should know how you behave when you are fine and when you are angry. Develop a sign, word of signal that they will give you when they notice you are losing your calm.

Some of the signs and words you may use include: a tap on the shoulder, a wave of the hand, a question like 'are you okay' or a simple request such as "lets breath."

Normally, the first reaction when you see the signal is denial, reflexively believing that you are not angry. Try to avoid a defensive state. Lifeguards are very objective therefore will see the weaknesses sooner than you.

Incentivize yourself.

After a relapse, it is important that you incentivize yourself. Motivation can come from making a list of the reasons why you want to change. Identify the three reasons that dominate your life for instance if you have lost too many friends, or you have embarrassed yourself too much thus looking for ways to protect further damage. Keeping these reasons in mind will help you get back up. You may identify many reasons but pick the top three or five to help you get back up. Stop and reflect on every goal and the importance of your plan.

Warning Signs of a Relapse

The following warning signs can help you identify when a regression is about to occur:

1. **The return of denial** - This involves the inability to recognize and tell other people what you are feeling

and thinking. This denial can happen even when you are unable to acknowledge that a slip up is coming, and you are failing back to the aggressive behavior.

2. **Apprehension about wellbeing** - This refers to the lack of confidence in your ability to control anger. It can happen when you find yourself in an aggravating scenario and have a hard time controlling yourself

3. **Defensiveness** - When a relapse is coming along, there are chances that you will take a defensive stand when talking about yourself. This often happens when you do not want to admit that you are sliding back to the old habits.

4. **Crisis building** - You will feel overwhelmed by life and an inability to control things. You will also feel that two more issues appear every time you sort out one. This will often occur if your plans are too stressful or demanding.

5. **Avoidance** - This involves avoiding the fact that something can make the former uncomfortable and painful feelings to come back. Consequently, you will find yourself avoiding the people and places that can make you engage in introspection.

6. **Immobilization** - This involves the feeling that you are not engaging effectively with other [people. It is more like you are just going through the motions of life. None of your problems feel like they are really solved and you will spend more time daydreaming rather than looking for solutions.

7. **Irritability** - This involves overreacting to small matters and losing your temper quickly. Irritability will occur more if you are disappointed with yourself and feeling frustrated.

8. **Plans begin to fail** - You will notice that most of your projects are not coming through more so because you are not following them up. For instance, if you had plans to stick to a healthy diet. You will find that you are junking a lot. This happens when you feel that the plans are too difficult and tiring

9. **Depression** - This will be represented by some major symptoms such as lack of sleep, Irregular eating habits, loss of interest in things that were former fun for you, and loss of a regular pattern in life. You may also feel that staying angry is the only way to let go of the depression

10. **Open rejection of help** - Another indication of relapse it rejection of aid. In most cases, the people around you will reach out and state their concerns about you. However, denial will make you reject their expressions.

11. **Inability to control your behavior** - This can manifest itself in an attitude of "I don't care." You will find yourself failing to attend to important matters such as meetings.

12. **Conscious lying** - This involves explaining away the truth and instead, selling lies about a situation.

13. **Spending more time with self-destructive and depressed people** - This can be an indicator or a result of a relapse. Initially, your recovery plan involved spending time with people who handle their anger in a healthy way. However, during relapse, you feel the need to spend more time with angry and depressed people.

Chapter 12: Anger Medication and Side Effects

Anger is a psychological issue—therefore, it is possible for one to treat the symptoms with medication. The goal of anger management programs is to help the person become self-sufficient—and while therapy is the best option, medication can help in the treatment phase.

Common Medications

Some medicine is known to prevent rage outburst and reduce aggression. They do not target the specific anger in the body; rather, they bring about a calming effect which controls the reactions. There are antidepressants, mood stabilizers and anti-psychotic drugs that help the patient to deal with anger but they hardly stop it completely.

Anti-Depressants

These drugs have been found to treat anger resulting from a number of mental disorders such as personality disorders and depression. Researchers found that anti-depressants made anger to disappear in 53-71 percent for depressed patients. The antidepressants used include imipramine, sertraline, and Fluoxetine.

Mood Stabilizers

In most Cases, anti-depressants are preferred when treating anger in people with other conditions such as depression and personality disorders because they are effective for the majority of the patients. However, there are cases where the antidepressant drugs fail; thus other medications such as mood stabilizers are recommended. Some anti-seizure medications such as carbamazepine and divalproex are used as stabilizers.

Antipsychotic Drugs

Researches show that some typical antipsychotic drugs such as Clozapine can be used to treat Schizophrenic patients who have aggressive and hostile behavior. Researchers explain that the drugs reduce anger because of their ability to minimize impulsivity. However, other studies state that though the antipsychotic drugs are effective with anger management, there are many side effects thus making then unviable for long term treatment.

The Safety of Medication Treatment

Evidently, medication is sometimes the best way to control anger in the short run. With the help of other treatment forms such as therapy, a patient might not need medication for too long. A professional may recommend certain drugs for long term use if they have little to no side effects. Of course, all medication comes with a risk. There are chances of addiction or other adversities.

It is important for one to take all medication as prescribed by the doctor or professional. Look out for any side effects and communicate with your doctor/ therapist. Doctors may do follow up checkups for that medication that have some risks. Closely monitor any adverse changes. It is also important for one to consult the therapist/doctor before coming off any anger medication.

Those people who have doubts about medication but still want to heal their anger challenges may seek help in alternative treatments such as essential oils and herbs along with therapy. Chamomile is one of the herbs used by people to calm their nerves down. Practices such as daily exercise, mindfulness, and meditation can help a patient to find calm and balance. However, it takes patience and a lot of persistence to achieve it.

Chapter 13: Summary of Anger Management Techniques

Feeling Angry

We all feel angry at one point or the other. Some people can deal with anger pretty quickly, but others have a harder time sorting irritability. We look at challenges from different angles and thus get different perspectives and results. Anger can lead to major complications in our lives and of those around us.

Anger normally informs us of when something may be wrong. For instance, we may feel at a loss when something is not within our control. Sometimes, anger helps us to avoid real feelings. If we are feeling afraid, anger helps us to feel confident and energetic enough to fight. Too much stress could also lead to anger. Stress makes us feel edgy; therefore, a little thing can force us to react very drastically.

Anger involves a wide array of feelings. It can be a little annoying because of a minor accident such as forgetting to pick milk at the store, or a form of rage because of a more serious issue such as seeing someone you love getting hurt. We all react depending on how we interpret the situation and the current state of mind. In some cases, one may feel angry for a reason he/she cannot identify.

Anger will be stronger for you if:
- It shows in a way that is stronger than you expected based on the situation;

- It occurs too frequent to the extent that you no longer enjoy life;
- It is caused by something that happened to you in the past, and you have not yet sorted it out;
- It results in violent acts towards someone else, property or to yourself;
- It is interfering with your ability to work;
- It is hurting your relationships or making people stay away from you; and
- It is affecting your health, physical, mental, and emotional.

What to Do

In some situation, everyone is forced to react in anger. This emotion can be helpful in some cases. For instance, as seen earlier, if anger makes you leave an abusive relationship, then it is good. It is healthy if the anger motivates you to take action on something or to work towards your goals. However, if one is dealing with anger in an unhealthy way, then it will lead to problems that can affect many sectors of life. Luckily there are some things that one can do to deal with anger.

Immediate Strategies

Immediate strategies will not solve the problem, but they help to put a person back in control. When one is in control, he/she is in a position to find productive ways to deal with the challenge. The immediate strategies will also help one to stay away from actions and words that he/she regrets later.

First, leave the situation that is making you angry if possible. Stepping away from the situation of anger can help you to relax and think in a clearer way. Remember that the reaction of the body when you are in a state of anger hinders one from taking all the things into consideration. Step away.

Secondly, count to ten. This applies more if you are in a situation where you can walk away without a proper reason for instance when talking to an employer. The best option is to count to ten slowly; this way, you will have time to moderate the anger.

Thirdly, repeat a calming phrase of choice. You can use words that bring peace to you such as 'stay calm' or peace and kindness. It would also help if you allow your brain to wander off to thoughts such as "will it matter in two months?"

Fourthly, take a deep breath and relax. Remember the breathing and relaxation techniques we talked about earlier? They come in handy at moments of urgency. Breathe in deeply to the stomach and release slowly, when taking in air, think of it as positive energy. When breathing out, think of it like you are letting go of the negative energy. Deep breaths help you to calm down your racing mind, lower the blood pressure and even slow the heart rate.

Fifthly, shift your attention. It might sound as disrespect or arrogance but it better than letting your anger hang out. Get your focus away from the subject matter and think of something pleasant. Identify something that you are looking forward to, such as a massage, or a fresh slice of cake. Whatever makes you happy, go for it.

Short-Term Strategies

Once the immediate strategies have helped you get a grip of the basic emotion, there are strategies that you can use to analyze the situation. The help you assess the emotions that flew about in the situation. These strategies do not take long, but when applied well, they can make a great difference.

Firstly, acknowledge the anger. If you keep denying the anger, you will not have the opportunity to deal with them. Anger will not go away just because you bottle them up. Acknowledgment and acceptance are the first steps to finding help for your problem.

Secondly, consider if the reaction was warranted by the situation. Anger is a normal part, but it becomes challenging if the reaction is too much for the situation. Consider what you would think if you saw someone else getting angry for the safe situation you were in. You may also ask someone you trust to help you check if the anger was warranted.

Thirdly, assess your thoughts. Mostly, anger is triggered by our thoughts. The way you perceive a circumstance determines the way you will react to it. It is therefore important that you assess the thoughts/feelings that you had while angry. Were they true or false?

Fourthly, identify the source of anger. Is it the words or actions of the other person that made you feel angry? Did they fail to do something? Try to deal with the source in a productive and peaceful way. Assertive skills can help you to sort the matter.

Fifthly, look for humor in the situation. You might have forgotten how to make humor out of a small matter.

Longer-Term Strategies

You might be looking for ways to sort your anger problem completely. Long term anger management strategies will take more effort and time, but they will help you to cope with your anger in different situations. The aim is to change the ways you handle anger so that it does not cause problems.

Firstly, learn the things that trigger your anger. While some people get angry because of other people such as their bosses, spouses or friends, others get angry because of the situations they cannot change such as traffic jams and missed planes. There are also people who lose their temper when they feel emotional for instance when they feel ashamed, angry, or guilty.

Secondly, identify your warning signs. Knowing your anger warning signs will help you to take action before losing your temper entirely. You need to avoid full-blown anger; therefore, catch it early enough. Some of the early signs of anger include tightening of the chest, irritability, resentment, palpitation, and feeling like lashing out.

Thirdly, talk to a person you trust. Try to get a second opinion from someone you know cannot get biased. Keep in mind that anger actually informs you of things that need change. Another person can help you to identify the real problem, identify solutions and even test them.

Fourthly, learn from other people. If your anger is from a situation that you cannot control such as a job, ask other people how they went about it. How did your coworker deal with a similar situation?

Fifthly, practice healthy thinking. Remember that anger is mostly triggered by our thoughts. Learn how to solve problems, think positively and manage stress. Do not assume that every person is out to make your life hard. Think critically and seek counsel.

Sixthly, physical activities have been identified as some of the helpful management strategies for many disorders. You could probably go for a walk, clean the house or play your favorite sport. This will help you to feel less tensed and forget.

Seventh, practice mindfulness. This involves practices such as meditation, which help you to look at your thoughts without judgment. This practice will help you to look at your anger and to also accommodate it without pushing it away.

Eighth, learn to be assertive. Assertiveness is one technique that helps one to manage anger. Learn how to communicate and act assertively. Remember that assertiveness does not stand for aggressiveness. Assertiveness is not pushy and demanding. Instead, it involves communicating your thoughts without pulling down or belittling other people. Make sure that your message is clear.

Ninth, let other people be. If your anger rises because of other people, for instance, your spouse or boss, remember that you cannot control them and they do not always have to act as you want. Their behavior is not your responsibility to a large extent.

Tenth, pick a treatment program. There are many programs available for use either as an individual or in a group. Pick one that fits your time and goals. Remember that although the programs designed for an individual are good, it is better if you use group therapy. It will offer you a better support system.

Remember that anger might signify another problem such as anxiety or depression. Talk to a professional.

Conclusion

Thank you for making it to the end of the book! We hope that you found it helpful and informative. Every effort was put to ensure that all the chapters could give you valuable information. We intentionally used simple language to make sure that every person reading it gets empowered. The book has deliberately avoided complicated theories and stuck to simple practices that one can use at their convenience.

The moment you understand anger is the moment that it becomes easier to deal with. Anger management is essential in everyday life. This book has taken you through the topic of anger management. There is no one specific thing that a person can do to manage anger overnight. However, if you follow the right steps, with dedication and commitment, you will get the results you seek. Combine a number of treatment options if need be. If you are working with a therapist, follow all the instructions he/she gives you and keep an open communication channel.

The next step is to stop reading and start applying the lessons in real life. Do whatever you have identified as necessary to curb anger and ensure the health and wellness of you and the people around you. You will find that many people are still ignorant about the proper ways of anger management. You will realize that the majority of those who seem to have it all together are just suppressing anger, and it will harm them in the end. To that end, try to engage them and teach them a thing or two you have learned herein. You may even recommend or gift this book to them.

You might also need to refer to this book at a later date. Keep it and review it as often as you want. Just because you have reached the end of the book does not mean that there is nothing else to learn about anger and its management. Read more and expand your horizons. It is the only way you will achieve the mastery you seek. Pay attention to the changes that will surround your life as soon as you start managing our anger, more so assertively. Use some of the tips herein to make the world a better place.

Description

What is anger? Why does anger lead many people to aggressive and unhealthy behavior? Does it have adverse physiological and psychological effects? Can we term all anger as negative?

Do you feel too irritable or on edge? Do traffic jams get you angry? Do your coworkers or boss easily anger you?

Untreated and uncontrolled anger can have very adverse effects on your physical, mental, and emotional health. It can take a toll on you and the people around you. Anger can also affect your relationships, career, family life, and even your general lifestyle.

In most cases, we suppress anger with the hope that it will not affect us and our relations, but that is not an effective way of dealing with it. You cannot ignore the emotion of rage forever—at one point, it will affect you. It's best if you recognize it, accept it, and deal with it. Put yourself in a position where anger does not run your life. Learn how to use the energy it gives in positively.

This book will help you to understand anger, guide you to identify your triggers of anger, and learn how to manage it. Managing anger can be very complicated if one does not have the right guidelines. To that end, this book uses a simple language to explain the helpful and unhelpful forms of anger. It also describes the steps that you can use to manage it.

Inside, you will find:

- The definition of anger;
- An expression of anger;
- Understanding anger and smart anger;
- The causes, signs, and symptoms of anger;
- What is unmanaged anger;
- The cost of anger;
- Anger and mental health;
- The choice to manage anger;
- Steps to managing anger effectively;
- Anger management and communication;
- Selecting a good anger management program;
- The use of anger management techniques; and
- Relapses and medication.

www.ingramcontent.com/pod-product-compliance
Lightning Source LLC
Chambersburg PA
CBHW071351080526
44587CB00017B/3062